Teaching Common Sense

Seven Simple Principles For Nuturing Those Around You and Reaping the Harvest of Your Life

Rhonda S. Jones

Bright Hope Productions

Requests for such permission should be addressed to:
Bright Hope Productions
Post Office Box 50730
Knoxville, Tennessee 37950

Jones, Rhonda S.
　　Teaching Common Sense:
　Seven Simple Principles For Nuturing Those Around You and Reaping the Harvest of Your Life

Cover Design: Mary Fisher Design
Layout: J. L. Saloff
Illustrations: Joe and Donna Marek
Fonts: Goudy, Italia Book, Book Antiqua

Perfectbound ISBN: 0-9766624-0-X
Library of Congress Control Number: 2005902090
Copyright information available upon request.

First Edition

Printed on acid-free paper in The United States of America.

This book is dedicated to
my sister, Rita, who always
believed in me,

and to

Tom who taught me to
believe in myself.

Table of Contents

Our lives are a continuing journey,
and we must learn and grow at every bend.
As we make our way, we can simply do our best,
sometimes stumbling but always
moving toward the finest within us.

—Capt. Gerald Coffee

Table of Contents

Acknowledgments ix

Introduction 11

Part I – What Is Teaching Common Sense?

Chapter 1: The Teaching Mystery Solved 25

Chapter 2: Teachers I Have Known 59

Part II – How Does Teaching Common Sense Work?

Chapter 3: The Seven Commonsense Principles of
Effective Teaching 89

Chapter 4: How My Good Teachers Did It 111

Part III – How Can I Practice Teaching Common Sense?

Chapter 5: The Teacher You Already Are 135

Chapter 6: The Teacher You Could Be 187

Chapter 7: The Universal Cure 237

For Further Information 243

Acknowledgments

It isn't what you know that finally counts;
it's who you are. – J. Brouwer

Rhonda Jones

Acknowledgments

From the youngest age I can recall, I was taught to think and *figure things out*. As a result of that mantra, repeated over and over again by my parents, I have now spent a few decades figuring things out. Input gathered by observing others and absorbing ideas and theories has blended into my own brand of commonsense wisdom. Therefore, this book would not have been possible without the contributions of my parents who taught me to think for myself, of the many great people who have passed through my life that I write about in these pages, and of the many well-known scientists, doctors, teachers, philosophers, religious leaders, activists, and schools of thought that I have studied.

Among the latter is Roger Sperry. His work informed my understanding of what happens in the two hemispheres of the human brain. Most modern-day understanding of left and right brain function stems from Sperry's brilliant Physiology & Science Nobel Prize-winning studies of 1981. By comparing cognitive abilities between the two severed brain halves of epileptic patients, Sperry found it was as if two separate brains were housed within a single cranial unit. The left brain, for example, was found to be superior to the right in tasks involving analytical, sequential, and linguistic processing, while the right performed better in holistic, parallel, and spatial abilities.

Tom Bird's work expands on this by describing how the left and right brain are in a continual leadership struggle, which is of particular interest to anyone engaged in artistic expression. And Bob Weyant's writing and teaching exposes the effects of being led by the left brain on our human interactions.

From the work of Marcus Buckingham, Donald Clifton, and their colleagues, I learned about the unique synapses formed in each individual's brain that result in innate talents. They describe the process whereby synapses are built between neurons in the brain from birth through the mid-teens. Through these synapses, an individual's talents—their range of stronger connections—are established. Based upon this phenomenon, Buckingham and Clifton define talents as any recurring pattern of thought, feeling, or behavior that can be productively applied. They argue that even something like obstinacy, which might be considered a frailty under certain circumstances, can still be a talent or strength if productively applied in the appropriate situation.

The mysteries of human development, utilizing this complex brain power and talents, have been further clarified for me by the writing of Abraham Maslow, Carl Jung, and Erik Erikson, three doctors who specialized in the study and practice of how people develop and grow psychologically.

Maslow popularized the concept of self-actualization. After studying several successful individuals, who seemed to have achieved the life they were born to live, Maslow concluded that there actually exists a hierarchy of needs a person must fulfill before this pinnacle of human existence can be reached. The first two levels of need in Maslow's hierarchy, physiological and safety, are quite synonymous with the dinosaur left brain described by Bob Weyant. While our dinosaur brain drives the survival instinct we share with the entire animal kingdom, under Maslow's theory it is the higher levels of need—love, esteem, and self-actualization—that separate us from the animals. The difference between Maslow's theory and that of predecessors like Freud and Skinner was that his hierarchy of needs recognized the uniqueness of each individual. Maslow claimed this process was characterized by the continual emergence and satisfaction of higher level needs.

Maslow wrote, "At once other (and higher) level needs emerge, and these, rather than physiological hungers, dominate the organism. And when these in turn are satisfied, again new (and still higher) needs emerge, and so on. As one desire is satisfied, another pops up to take its place."

Erik Erikson's work describes this progress through eight predictable stages of psychosocial development. Beginning at birth, with the infant learning a sense of trust or distrust of him or herself, his or her parents, and the world, the stages progress through pre-school, adolescent, and typical school years.

The stages continue even after the body reaches the apex of its physical development and begins its inevitable physical decline. Then dawns the awareness that furthers the psychological development, which continues throughout the stages of physical decline. The strong innate desire for deep inner unity drives lifelong learning in the pursuit of becoming a unique but unified person. Until finally at the culmination of life in the final stage, we are faced with the finality of life and evaluate our life and accomplishments to affirm that our life has been meaningful.

Healthy resolution of all eight of the psychosocial development stages, according to Erikson, results in a sense of integrity and satisfaction that one's life has left an indelible mark.

The fifth of Erikson's stages of psychosocial development has particular relevance to my beliefs and is focused on achieving a sense of identity to eliminate a sense of confusion in one's life. Successful resolution of the identity crisis that typifies this stage is necessary, as is the resolution of the crises in all the other stages, before an individual's development can continue. Psychiatrist's and psychologist's offices are filled with people who are stuck in one of these stages dealing with old issues and unresolved crises, which are preventing them from moving on. They are recreating and reliving these same crises in all their choices and interactions over and over again in a desperate spiral. Resolution is critical to their happiness.

Carl Jung, a Swiss psychiatrist and founder of analytic psychology who lived from 1875 to 1961, called this lifelong process individuation, characterized by the pursuit to unify the conscious and unconscious mind in order to be the most fulfilled humans we can be. His work reveals the degree to which humans suppress feelings, thoughts, emotions, memories, tendencies, and talents in their subconscious or even deeper in the shadow of their unconscious mind.

Jung's writing regarding the awakenings that typify midlife has also influenced me. He described how human existence is governed by five functions: thinking, feeling, sensing, perceiving, and spiritual. Everyone has a superior function that controls his or her thoughts and actions. The popular Myers-Brigg Personality Type Index is constructed around the determination of whether an individual is primarily thinking, feeling, sensing or perceiving in nature. Jung documented how, while individuals are typically governed by one of these functions, humans typically begin to strive in midlife for more balance across all five functions by becoming more conscious of their behavior.

Jung developed this popular theory involving the unconscious mind and what he referred to as archetypes after years of research. Archetypes, according to his findings, are the biologically inherited patterns, symbols, images, and motifs that have been passed through the collective unconscious of the species for millenniums.

For instance, there is an innate knowing we all possess for what it means to be male or female. When a woman becomes a mother for the first time, she instinctively knows to care for and protect her offspring, due to this archetype embedded in her genetic code. It is unconscious until needed, then called into action in the conscious mind. Jung found preeminent among these archetypal images in the human unconscious mind was the God-image. He found that people from all cultures down through time have been inclined to believe in the divine. Jung focused his professional work on the psychological aspect of this discovery, but in his private letters and ancillary writings, he explored the metaphysical perspective. There he expressed a more spiritual understanding of something that we are all somehow tapped into. Jung referred to God as the "mightiest force in the psyche." Based upon direct experience, through his many years of work with the God-image in the human psyche, Jung reported, ". . . we find numberless images of God . . . there is no doubt in my mind that there is an original behind our images." Jung's theory, proven by years of work that remains the foundation of psychotherapy, could be interpreted to say that humans are wired to believe in God—that is, a creator, a higher power, a source. And we remain connected, however tightly or loosely, with that source through the deepest part of our psyche.

As a result, these medical and scientific theories go hand in hand with my ideas about the purpose for each life, which has grown out of a lifetime of Christian education and exposure to religious authors and teachers, such as Rick Warren. I was first introduced to the principles of choice and accountability through that Christian education, which stresses the concept of a loving God who gives us choices.

The Old Testament story in the Bible of Samuel, found in I Samuel 3, introduces the corresponding principle of accountability. It recounts how a young Samuel, who would grow to be one of the greatest leaders in Israel, is awakened from his slumber by a voice calling out to him. Three times Samuel mistakes this voice for the call of his father. But each time he finds that his father, Eli, is asleep. Still the voice called and spurred him to action.

In this way, the Bible scholars explain, the age of accountability is a time when we become adults and do not need our fathers to give direction anymore. It is the time when we hear our own voice of reason, or in this case hear the voice and direction of God. It is a time when we make our own choices, including not heeding the voice, which is also in itself a choice. It is a time when we become accountable for the outcome of our choices.

My religious foundation has been complemented by a study of all the great philosophers down through history. These religious tenets and philosophical theories have combined to sharpen my belief about the meaning of this life, which has been further enhanced by the work of James Redfield. Redfield's focus on the spiritual nature of this existence has coupled well with my religious background and philosophical and scientific study to form a foundation for my all-encompassing theory of life, which is a balance of both the scientific and spiritual.

Redfield also cites the works of many scientists, philosophers, and religious leaders to posit that we are actually spiritual beings having a human experience. Redfield convincingly describes how throughout history human beings have been subconsciously struggling to implement this lived spirituality on Earth. In his popular *Celestine Insights*, he describes individuals who experience the journey of their lives as a spiritual unfolding. Certainly, we could extrapolate from Redfield's theory that our desire is fueled by our innate need to make this human experience as rich as possible before returning to our spiritual origins.

Redfield's work is supported by that of Margaret Wheatley to provide enlightenment about the interconnectedness of all creation and all people, one to another. Margaret Wheatley's work applied the quantum physics theory to understanding leadership of people and organizations.

She points out that energy particles do not exist independently of their relationship to one another and neither do human beings. There is power and energy hidden in the invisible fields that surround and connect us all. According to Redfield, the realization that we live in a universe of dynamic energy is contributing to a more complete worldview that opens us up to the real nature of our universe and the real purpose of human life on this planet. Through connection to this sacred energy, we can discover our own growth path in life and our spiritual mission—the personal way we can contribute to the world. This new physics, referenced by Redfield and Wheatley, describes the world in terms of a quantum field of energy comprising everything.

My understanding of how all these connected people struggle to survive . . . achieve . . . and fulfill their purpose, both individually and in groups, grew out of the work of not only Redfield and Wheatley, but also such notables as Thomas Kuhn, Peter Senge, Bob Weyant, Stephen Covey, Robert Carkhuff, and Bernard Berenson.

I have been heavily influenced by Thomas Kuhn's theory of paradigms and Peter Senge's similar theory of mental models. Senge, Director of the Systems Thinking and Organizational Learning Program at MIT's Sloan School of Management, also alludes in his book, *The Fifth Discipline*, to key coaching behaviors that facilitate learning. These concepts have helped validate my thoughts about coaching to influence others to challenge their paradigms, learn, and grow.

Bob Weyant writes about influencing others, based in part on the research of Robert Carkhuff and Bernard Berenson. Weyant teaches us how to demonstrate the core dimensions of respect, empathy, genuineness, and specificity or concreteness, which were proven by Carkhuff and Berenson's research to be critical helping behaviors. Weyant also builds on this base to teach personal accountability, which is recognizing that each choice results in either a positive or negative natural consequence for which we must accept accountability if we are to learn and grow.

Stephen Covey also writes and teaches about the power of choice. Covey is an internationally respected leadership authority, family expert, teacher, organizational consultant, speaker, and bestselling author. In his *Lessons in Leadership* series, Covey claims that leadership is a choice, not an organizational position, and involves communicating value so clearly to the people in your circle of influence that they come to see it in themselves. Valuing others, working to create a world in which individuals can flourish, and helping them develop a liberating awareness of the power of personal accountability has a particular appeal for me.

From the Humanism school of thought and the lives and teaching of individuals such as Myles Horton and Martin Luther King, Jr., I have clarified my beliefs about the sin and the tragedy of inaction in that regard. The ideas presented in this book, with regard to the reciprocal nature of sacrificing self to help others as the pathway for actually fulfilling self, are demonstrated in the lives of such individuals.

Humanism is a school of thought around which much debate continues over whether it is philosophy or religion. There are different types of humanism, depending on which side of this philosophical divide they fall. Humanism first emerged in ancient Greece with the Stoics who drew attention to human fellowship. Renaissance Humanism developed at the end of the Middle Ages and represented a spirit of human learning with the ability to determine truth for themselves. Philosophical Humanism is an outlook on life, which developed later centered on human need and interest, with the subcategories of Christian Humanism and Secular Humanism. Christian Humanism embraces self-fulfillment within the framework of Christian principles, while Secular Humanism chooses to reject the supernatural, opting for a more naturalistic and scientific framework. Yet their foundation is common. All forms of humanism teach of the immorality of inaction. Humanist Kenneth Phifer declares, "We have powers of a remarkable kind. We have a high degree of choosing what we will do."

Martin Luther King, Jr. and Myles Horton chose from a very young age to fight for the rights of the oppressed. Horton, born in Savannah, Tennessee, in 1905, began the Highlander education program in the mountains of Tennessee in 1932. Highlander Folk School, modeled after the folk schools of Denmark, under Horton's direction played a pivotal role in both the labor movement of the 1930s and 40s and the Civil Rights movement of the 50s and 60s. Horton and his associates started literacy programs for poor, southern African-Americans, so they could vote. At Highlander School, founded by Myles Horton, Civil Rights movement leaders like Martin Luther King, Jr. and Rosa Parks were trained in the methods of peaceful resistance, before Mrs. Parks' now-famous refusal to give up her seat in the front of the bus. Renamed the Highlander Research and Education Center, the organization settled into its current home in New Market, Tennessee, during the 1970s and continues to be a major catalyst for social change in the United States, despite Myles Horton's death in 1990. Notable figures, including Eleanor Roosevelt who visited the school on occasion, befriended Horton and Highlander. Because of Myles Horton, many who struggled against injustice were supported in their efforts to take collective action and shape their own destiny . . . to fulfill their life's purpose. Thanks to the well-publicized efforts of King, an entire country was moved to a higher level of existence.

Finally, from the theories of teachers and philosophers like Plato, Socrates, Carl Rogers, Paulo Freire and Jack Mezirow, I have learned how to help others learn and grow. The approach of these teachers involved exposing others to what they didn't know they didn't know.

Plato's *Allegory of the Cave* has been an ever-present metaphor for me. It describes people who were kept in a cave, their hands and feet bound, as they sat facing the back wall. Outside the mouth of the cave, a huge fire burned in front of which people carried stick figures back and forth. The captives had been watching these shadows reflected on the back wall of the cave for so long, they were unable to distinguish between this distorted version of life and the real thing.

One day one of the captives finally loosened his bonds and walked out of the cave to find the truth. He saw the fire and the illusions and the beautiful world full of possibilities beyond the cave. His old paradigm was shattered, replaced by a new more-enlightened one. He then returned, where he spent the rest of his life unsuccessfully trying to change the hardened, although incorrect, paradigm of those still in the cave.

I have seen this represented as a pie of three unequal slices. The pie represents the sum total of all that can be known. The three slices represent (1) what we know we know, (2) what we know we don't know, and (3) what we don't know we don't know.

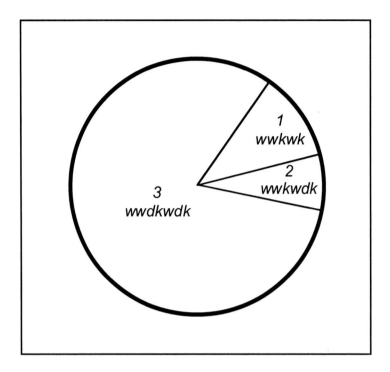

The goal, of course, is to expand section one, *what we know we know,* by shrinking sections two and three, especially section three, *what we don't know we don't know.*

From Carl Roger's writing, I learned that the facilitation of significant learning and change rests on the quality of the personal relationship between the teacher and the learner. Both Carl Rogers, noted psychologist, and Malcolm Knowles, referred to as the father of modern adult education, are well known for the view that the appropriate role for a teacher is that of a facilitator. Tennant and Pogson, in *Learning and Change in the Adult Years,* claim that the relationship between teachers and learners should be participative and democratic and characterized by openness, mutual respect, and equality.

Paulo Freire, the Brazilian educator who had a considerable impact on the development of informal educational practice, emphasized dialogue, people working with each other, and building community to facilitate learning. He was concerned with leading people to take informed action, which he called praxis. He grounded his education in the lived experience of the individuals he was trying to help and was concerned that they develop a level of consciousness—a process he called conscientization—that has the power to transform reality.

Similarly, Jack Mezirow focused on transformative learning brought on by disorienting dilemmas, which are situations that do not fit into preconceived notions. These dilemmas prompt critical reflection on beliefs, attitudes, opinions, and emotional reactions and result in the development of new ways of interpreting experiences. From these and other theories, I came to understand and appreciate the methods and practices by which we learn and grow.

This book would not have been possible without these contributions and their effect on my current thinking, nor would my life have been so full and rewarding. For that, I am eternally grateful.

Rhonda Jones

Introduction

To acquire knowledge, one must study;
but to acquire wisdom, one must observe.
– Marilyn Vos Savant, Writer

Introduction

Why did I write this book, and why should you listen to what I have to say? That is a very good question.

While I was facilitating a focus group in an adult education Master's program, one of the students—a pastor of a church—made the claim that after taking these classes, he still did not know how to teach. His comment surprised me, but what surprised me even more was how badly I wanted to stop and explain the secret to him. It was as if in that moment every word I had ever read or heard spoken and every experience I had ever had—all those facts, theories, memories and trivia—organized into a logical, clear message that begged to be delivered.

The desperate look in that student's eyes expressed a need that I soon realized is not limited to those who want to be teachers. I see that same look all the time on the faces of many who seem to be flip-flopping between self-assuredness and confusion. That was when I realized this book is not just an answer to a question from a student. This book is not only for teachers. This book is for everyone who wants to know the secret to living the life you were born to live. I wrote this book because I can't sit back, watching everyone wander through this life dazed and confused, and not do my part to fix it.

That is what we did on the farm where I grew up. We fixed things. There was no repairman to call. We had to be carpenter, plumber, electrician, veterinarian, and mechanic. When something broke, we had to fix it with whatever we had on hand. That must be why we never threw anything away. I mean nothing . . . not a piece of rope, a scrap of electrical cord, an old bucket with a hole in it, a strand of wire, or a torn fan belt. Even if we never were able to use it again for its original purpose, we might use it to satisfy some other need in the future. This is a practice that has influenced me more than I ever expected. I guess subconsciously I never threw anything away in my mind either. And I stubbornly refuse to believe that all I have endured has not been for a reason. All those things I have heard, seen, and lived through—good and bad—have all been put to good use in this book. They were always there, like the rope and wire hanging in the tool shed, waiting to be used . . . waiting for the need to arise, which they could satisfy. Now I recognize the need. I see too many people messing up and missing the wonderful chance to live the life they were born to live. I want to fix it. And I realize now that I have spent my whole life preparing for this job. I have not only lived through it; I have also studied it further in the adult education Master's program. I not only believe the concepts put forth in this book to be true. I know they are true. These solutions stem from the realization that life is a combination of teaching and learning. I am going to use everything in my tool shed to show you how to do that and to help you understand that this is the path to living the life you were born to live.

Hiking through the forest the other day, I was awe-inspired by the unusual rock formations. Weathered by years of wind and water, they possessed a sort of otherworld look to them. Smooth and rounded in some places, pockmarked and dimpled in others, they reminded me of an acne-scarred complexion. In some places, running water had dissolved the sandstone, leaving behind the exposed iron ore. The exposure of these crinkled veins to air left behind a rusty oxidation and verde patina, resembling a slice of rotting cabbage.

One could easily look upon these mountains of rock and see damage . . . a sad, ugly hill defeated by the elements. But what I saw was beauty. In fact, it is these very rock formations that draw hundreds of hikers to these trails. Despite the bombardment of weather over the years, these rocks stand tall and proud. Every assault has been endured. The rock has become pliable and has evolved itself in such a way that reveals its many treasures, like the iron ore hidden inside. Rock houses have formed, which have provided much needed shelter over the years for Native Americans, runaway slaves, and weary hikers. Natural bridges, carved into graceful arches, have transported foot travelers for decades. Smooth, round stone pools have formed to cradle the clear, life-giving spring water. The trials and tribulations of time have not destroyed the rock. They have beautified and enhanced it. Nothing has been wasted. Everything has been put to good use.

That is what the theory put forth in this book is about. Everything to which I have ever been exposed . . . everything to which you have ever been exposed . . . has had a purpose. It has all happened—the good and the bad—for a reason. It has happened to bring you ever closer to living the life you were born to live.

This book will prove that theory for you in the same manner it was proven to me . . . through my own experiences. I have weathered half a life to reach this point of clarification, and now desire to share it with you. I want you to reach that same clarity and inner peace. I want you to grow to appreciate those storms you, too, have weathered. I want you to recognize the treasures you have hidden inside. I want you to learn how to help others do the same. Read these pages and realize, as I have, that we all weather the storms of life and become beautified by them through a combination of teaching and learning. Recognize that being the best you can be at both is the path to not only being a good teacher, but also to true happiness and fulfillment. This book will not only show you how to be a successful teacher, if that is what you desire. Moreover, this book will show you how to live life.

In Greek philosophy there exists the theory of eudaimonism. According to this philosophy each individual has within a *daimon*—an inner spirit or genius of infinite value—that is unique to him or her. If the genius goes unrealized, then it is forever lost to the world. As a result, the joy of all humanity is diminished, for no other person will be able to make the exact same contribution of spirit and genius. You must succeed in living your genius.

Being successful is something for which we are all conditioned to strive. We may choose many different paths in that quest. We may define success by the careers we have, the houses we live in, the people we marry or with whom we associate, the cars we drive, the children we raise, and the possessions we acquire. There are as many different symbols of success as there are individual personalities. But these are merely that . . . symbols.

When you look beyond these symbols, success is not a place or a destination that we reach, nor is it a thing or even a collection of things we possess. Success is a state of being. It is the way we live our lives. It is not the way we are going to live our lives at some point in the future after we have finished certain activities or acquired certain possessions. Success is the way we live our lives now. The manner in which we go about each and every moment, regardless of wealth, social status, or career, is what being successful is all about.

This fact was never more clear to me than when I spent time at an orphanage in the mountains of Guatemala. Over five hundred poor, abused, orphaned and abandoned children, along with fifteen dedicated adults, call the orphanage home. Initially, I was struck by the deprivation.

Each child is issued two pair of pants, four shirts and one pair of shoes, which must be worn until threadbare, in order to stretch the meager donations in support of all the needy children. Even one toy per child is out of the question in this situation. They are lucky if they have a few toys to share amongst them. To these children, a piece of paper and a pencil, with which to draw a picture of a sunrise, is a treat. These children will carefully split one small piece of Starburst candy into six pieces to share with one another. I was overcome by how little they had in this environment.

When I stepped into this setting, nothing I had achieved in my life—none of the typical trappings of success—mattered anymore. No one knew what I did for a living, what kind of house I lived in, what kind of car I drove, or how much money or how many possessions I had amassed. None of that mattered. All of that was stripped away, and the only thing that mattered—the only thing I had that was of any use—was what was inside me. All I could do there was be my one true self and live the life I was born to live . . . to give those children whatever I could find inside of me to give . . . love, respect, empathy, genuineness, inspiration, hope.

When all that we confuse with success was stripped away, all that was left was to just be me and help those children, in whatever way I could, to be all that they could be. All that was left for me to do was to be a teacher to and a student of these children. That is what my theory is all about. Living the life you were born to live and being your one true self simply requires living your genius . . . sharing it with the world.

At the orphanage, I met a nineteen-year-old premed student named Byron, who was an eleven-year resident of the home. Knowing Byron taught me what it really means to realize your own genius. You see, Byron thought his value to the world was going to be through the medical field. For several years, while living in the orphanage, Byron was planning to be a doctor. But, while he was *planning* to be a doctor, what he was actually *doing* was connecting with and influencing the constant stream of *gringos* who visited the orphanage to do short- and long-term mission work. Byron's spirit shined through his sparkling eyes, and his warm, open personality reached out and connected with not only the visitors but also each child in the ever-growing population of the home. Byron served as a big brother and a role model to the other residents in the home and as an interpreter for all the visitors. Every person who arrived at the orphanage feeling sorry for the children, departed with an admiration for the size of these children's hearts and the strength of their character. We developed that enlightened perspective because of Byron and his unique ability to communicate so clearly to you what really mattered in their lives.

This boy taught me a great deal. He framed up what matters most in these succinct words. "What I need, I have; and what I do not have, I do not need." In that one comment from Byron, I resolved all the issues that had combined to lead me to this place. I learned what it means to live the life you were born to live, regardless of your circumstances. I learned what it means to give your inner value to the world. I learned what being successful really means. I learned that, while on the surface they seemed to have so little, in reality they have so much.

Two short months after I left the orphanage, Byron died in his sleep of a brain aneurysm. Hundreds of missionaries and current and former residents of the orphanage who were touched by Byron, as I had been, grieved his death. But, even as we mourned, one thing was abundantly clear. Byron's life, though short by most standards, was no tragedy.

Byron lived his genius every day and fulfilled his purpose. He touched more hearts and lives in his short nineteen years than many of us ever will. Like the rock formations in the mountains, the storms Byron weathered exposed his inner beauty. Byron was not limited by his situation. He turned it into the vehicle for being his one true self . . . for living the life he was born to live. Byron taught everyone with whom he came in contact how to do that too.

You see, it is all there . . . inside of you . . . waiting to be called into action. It does not matter where you are or what your situation is . . . how filled with plenty or scarcity it may be. You are here for a reason. You can fulfill that purpose. The power is within you. All that you need, you already have.

All you have to do is teach and learn. It is that simple. For life is simply a combination of being teacher and student. I have proven it in my life, and now I will teach you how to prove it in your own life. But why am I compelled to bring you that message through this book? That is another good question, which I will gladly answer.

It *is* simple. Yet learning it is not always easy. I have learned much of it the hard way, and so will you. Nevertheless, what you read in this book will turn those difficult experiences into the lessons they are intended to be on your path to becoming not only the best teacher you can be but also to becoming your one true self. A world in which everyone is striving for and achieving that level of fulfillment is the kind of world I want to help create.

Humanism tells us whatever our philosophy of the universe may be, ultimately the responsibility for the kind of world in which we live rests with us. Abraham Maslow was a Humanist, and his theory of self-actualization describes the natural quest of all mankind to live the life they were born to live, whether that means they will be a teacher, or an artist, or whatever. Many religious faiths reject the Humanist principles. However, neither Maslow's theory of self-actualization nor the various forms of Humanism completely eliminate a place for religious theory. Even though the work of Maslow stressed the expression of self, it still recognized the role religion can play. Maslow wrote, "The state of being without a system of values is psychopathogenic. The human being needs a framework of values, a philosophy of life, a religion or religion-surrogate to live by and understand by, in about the same sense he needs sunlight, calcium, and love."

When Maslow's theory and the Humanist philosophy on which it is based are applied to the idea of learning, it involves the development of a liberating awareness that enables an individual to achieve his or her highest potential. One of the basic principles of Maslow's theory is that the salvation of the human being is not found in the darker side of humanity on which his predecessors like Freud had focused, but rather in the questions of value, individuality, consciousness, purpose, ethics, and the higher reaches of human nature. He wrote that this salvation or self-actualization results in peak experiences, "feelings of limitless horizons opening up to the vision, the feeling of being simultaneously more powerful and also more helpless than one ever was before, the feeling of ecstasy and wonder and awe, the loss of placement in time and space with, finally, the conviction that something extremely important and valuable had happened, so that the subject was to some extent transformed and strengthened even in his daily life by such experiences."

This concept of salvation and peak experiences, in my opinion, link Maslow's theory and Humanism to Christianity. Christian religious principles include the belief that God has a purpose for each individual. Rick Warren, author of the popular book, *The Purpose-Driven Life*, claims that the Humanist question of "What do I want or need?" must be replaced with "What does God want for me?" According to Warren and all Christians like him, humans are created by and for God's purpose. The purpose of one's life fits into a much larger, cosmic purpose that God has designed for eternity.

Warren quotes the Bible wherein it says, "It is in Christ that we find out who we are and what we are living for. Long before we first heard of Christ and got our hopes up, he had his eyes on us, had designs on us for glorious living, part of the overall purpose he is working out in everything and everyone."

Warren and the many denominations of Christian religions posit that it is in God that we can discover our origin, identity, meaning, purpose, significance and destiny. They claim life is not about using God to achieve our own self-fulfillment, rather it is about letting God use us for the fulfillment of his purpose. Their position suggests that people are born with a "God-shaped hole" that creates a yearning designed to lead us in search of God.

Proponents of this Christian theory characterize those Humanist philosophies and resulting theories as self-centered and rejecting of God. But, at the same time, the Christian framework includes the concept of a spirit within each of us guiding us, leading us, toward the fulfillment of purpose . . . unique purpose . . . for each of us. For this reason, I see beyond the conflict between the two theories. I see the commonality that is integral to both sides of the argument. I can say that both sides of the debate are correct. Regardless of whether we believe a supreme being created us and preordained our unique purpose in life, or if we believe humans are supreme beings that create a life with purpose, the point remains.

We are all seeking the same pinnacle of existence . . . that same peak experience of living the life we were born to live. We learn more each and every day what that means and how to grow ever closer to the realization of it. That is what life is . . . a continual process, accelerated by our interactions with our environment, resulting in learning and peak experiences that confirm we are moving toward something . . . drawn toward that purpose-driven life . . . that salvation . . . that destiny.

If my environment, however, were an empty, white room, a virtual vacuum, within which I sat day after day, I probably would not learn much. The way we really learn and become our true selves is through interaction with others. I am learning from you at the same time that you are learning from me. I am your student, and you are my teacher. I am your teacher, and you are my student. It is human nature. We are social, relational animals. Our brains are always seeking the learning that leads to security in order to satisfy the dinosaur left brain, as well as the enlightenment and purpose that satisfies the right. The world and everyone and everything in it are my teachers. I am at once both student and teacher. It is a critical fact of our existence, this continual learning from one another, because we are here now, at this time, in this place, each of us, for a reason. Each and every life has a purpose.

As easy as that assertion is for me to make, it is equally easy to debate. It is not difficult to look around and see lives being lived that seem to lack any purpose at all. Many people seem to be moving without intent through the bland routines of one gray day after another. That is the problem. Lack of awareness and complacency are the diseases devouring our lives, our happiness and our potential. Those are the cancers this book is designed to cure.

My desire to present this cure to you stems from a deep desire, which I believe exists in each of us. Christians and those with similar religious beliefs trace this desire to a collective search for the kingdom of God. Following the pathways of their faith leads to that heaven. On the other hand, Humanists and similar secular-minded groups and individuals are following a path aimed at creating a sort of heaven on earth. In either case, there is an ultimate goal of a perfect existence, characterized by the joy of complete fulfillment and total fellowship.

In the Christian faith, the Bible teaches that Jesus has entrusted each of us with the ultimate eternity of all those around us. He obligated all those who follow his teaching to be diligent in their work to lead all people to the kingdom of heaven. Similarly, Humanists profess an all-encompassing obligation to help others create the best kind of world possible . . . to reach that fulfillment . . . to create that "heaven." Jesus issued that commission to his followers. In the Bible, Jesus' call for Christians to lead others is referred to as the great commission.

I realize that does not resonate with everyone. I learned that the hard way, too, a couple years ago when I e-mailed a Christmas blessing to my colleagues. It reminded all who read it to focus during the holiday season not on decorations, food, and social events, but rather on love of family. This particular blessing promoted showing love through hugging a child, kissing the spouse, being patient with children, not being envious of those who seemed to be having a more elaborate Christmas, and giving to those who are unable to reciprocate. It concluded by reminding the reader that we should celebrate this love of family and friends in this manner because it models the love God showed the world when he sent his son, Jesus, on Christmas morning.

By all accounts, I thought it was a typical Christmas card. But, almost immediately after I had pushed the send button, I received a challenging response from a colleague. He advised me that he is an agnostic who does not believe in Christ but has higher moral values than most so-called Christians, is a good person and has a very full life. He wanted to know if that meant my greeting did not apply to him . . . if I thought he did not deserve to enjoy the love and fellowship of which the blessing spoke.

This was the first time in my life that I had been challenged in such a manner on this topic. So, in that regard, it was a little surprising. Nevertheless, I knew just as quickly that I could not and would not withhold my best wishes from anyone, regardless of whether they shared my perspective. For this reason, I have attempted to write this book in such a way that does not ignore my beliefs, but also leaves room for all to benefit.

Therefore, this I believe with all my being. Regardless of whether or not you believe the source of that commission to help others toward fulfillment is spiritual or not, whether you believe the source of the power to carry out that commission is supernatural or very human, whether you believe it is the great commission of God or the great commission of Humanity, the same core truth remains. It is the common denominator . . . the common ground on which we all can stand. And that common truth is this. We each possess the power within us. Regardless of your motivation—spiritual or scientific, religious or secular—life simply is a combination of everyone being a student and a teacher, striving toward that eventual fulfillment of potential. Like the rock formations in the forest, we are all commissioned to weather the storms with grace, while we help others safely through as well.

There is a disease among us that is destroying our lives, our happiness and our potential. Ironically, curiosity about how to be a good teacher led me to that realization, and more importantly, it led me to the cure. If your neighbor had a terminal disease, and you had the cure, would you not race to give that cure to him or her? That is why this book had to be written. That is why you must read it.

Part I: What Is Teaching Common Sense?

We who lived in the concentration camps can remember men who walked through the huts comforting others, giving away their last piece of bread. They may have been few in number, but they offer sufficient proof that everything can be taken from a man but one thing: The last of his freedoms—to choose one's attitude in any given set of circumstances, to choose one's own way.

—Victor E. Frankl, *Man's Search for Meaning*

The Teaching Mystery Solved

We don't receive wisdom; we must discover it for ourselves
after a journey that no one can take for us or spare us.
– Marcel Proust

One

Ken was my boss in one capacity or another for about five years. It seems much longer than that, for in that short five years I attempted more, achieved more and grew more than I had in all the years of my career leading up to it. Why? It's because Ken not only believed in me and inspired me, he empowered me to do what I do best every single day.

When I went to work for Ken on the first project that brought us together, he didn't know anything about me. He was on the management development fast track and well on his way to a successful senior management career. I, on the other hand, was the experienced, albeit sheltered, country girl from the factory. That's where I had spent every day for the past fifteen years of my life, while finishing my education and enduring the ups and downs of young adulthood.

I felt pretty confident about my knowledge of the industrial side of the business. But I knew more about the factory than I did about myself. It had never occurred to me that I might be unique in any way or that I might have something special to offer the team. No one had ever looked beneath the competence I exhibited on the surface. In retrospect, it now seems that Ken started excavating those treasures from day one.

Ken soon discovered certain talents lying dormant in me and began to cultivate those talents. He would give me little side projects to do that required me to be creative. He asked me to help him think through important, high-level presentations he needed to make. Energized by his confidence, a hidden ability was awakened in me to craft a message, tell a compelling story, and mobilize the team around it. Witnessing the positive effects of my work and feeling the energy that flowed through this medium invigorated me.

On my own then I began seeking out the knowledge and skills that would hone this innate ability that I had unknowingly been carrying around for years. I'd always assumed that everyone was just like me. I was nothing special. Everyone noticed what I noticed . . . thought what I thought . . . felt what I felt. Under Ken's leadership I began to realize this wasn't true.

Enabled by Ken's enthusiasm and encouragement urging me on, I discovered that I possessed an insight into people that in some cases went beyond that of his other team members. This was my unique contribution. This was what made it possible for me to craft a compelling message. This was what made it possible for me to motivate project teams to success over whom I had no direct authority. Ken never held me back. If anything, he empowered me to pursue whatever I saw that needed attention. For the first time in my years working for this company, Ken made me realize that I was valuable.

One of the reasons I finally had this realization is because Ken, himself, told me so. He had this wonderful way of delivering the most heartfelt thank-you. On several occasions at staff Christmas parties or project completion celebrations, Ken would stand up in the middle of the room. He would look at us and, in front of the entire group, speak directly to each one of us.

In these personalized speeches, he would tell you how special you were. He would praise your unique talents and the particular contribution that you made to the team. To each one of us in turn, Ken would give credit for making him the manager that he was and for making the team as strong and successful as it was. Here was a senior executive of the company in front of his whole team making the proclamation that he owed his entire success to you.

It was not a trite, practiced speech. He did not read it. Ken spoke off-the-cuff, from his heart. He just stood up and talked to you. There was no doubt that it was sincere. It was always so moving that I would begin to cry as soon as he started with the first person in the room. By the time he got around to me, my tear-stained face looked as if I had been sitting through a marathon of chick-flicks. I shed tears of joy brought on by a man who was not insecure . . . was not intimidated . . . but was proud of and grateful for your abilities . . . honored that you were willing to apply them in pursuit of his mission.

What I am is good enough,
if I would only be it openly.
– Carl Rogers

It may seem strange that anyone could reach middle age and still need someone like Ken to encourage them to become the person they were born to be. The odd truth is that we all needed it. In my case, I had been taught throughout my childhood to be humble. Don't brag on yourself. Don't get the bighead. Don't show up other people. I had misinterpreted those messages and allowed them to confuse me into thinking I had to hold myself in check.

On the farm we had ducks whose wings we had to clip so they wouldn't fly away. Subconsciously, my wings were clipped too. It was always as if something inside me was trying to bubble up, but I was trained to keep it bottled inside. I never really questioned it, until I went to work for Ken. He wanted to bring all that out. He understood how valuable it is, and he wasn't worried about me showing him up by being able to do something he couldn't. His confidence in himself and in me gave me wings to fly.

After I had worked for Ken for a few years, I was talking to my sister about her intelligent young son. Tests at school had revealed him to be "academically gifted" and the administration was talking with her about the options for his continued development. She was asking me to help her weigh the options for keeping him in class with his friends while still keeping him challenged.

"I was talking to Daddy about it," she said, "and he was saying that was what they had to decide when you tested AG . . . whether to keep you in the mainstream or separate you for more challenging instruction. They decided to just keep you in the classroom and not say a word." She continued to talk, but I had stopped listening.

"What did you say?!" I was incredulous. "Did you say that I tested AG in grade school?" I was stunned.

"You mean you didn't know?!" Now it was her turn to be stunned.

Suddenly the laughter came bursting from inside me. "Well, they've sure done an excellent job of executing their plan, because I'm forty-one years old, and they haven't said a word about it yet!"

We laughed together and I realized that it doesn't matter now. My parents don't have to tell me. No one has to tell me because, thank goodness, Ken's leadership has shown me. "You're one of a kind, Rhonda!" Ken would always say with that sparkle in his eye and sincerity in his voice. Ken valued my uniqueness and, as a result, he set it free.

A few weeks ago on the occasion of Ken's departure from the company, we had a party. This time it was our turn to celebrate Ken. This was our time to look Ken in the eye and, in front of all our colleagues, tell him how special he is. On that night, this is the message I delivered to him: Ken, you connected with me as an individual, inspired me to see new possibilities, instilled unwavering commitment, provided structure within which I could learn and grow, gave me unconditional acceptance, believed in me, and set an example for me all along the way. You made me laugh, cry, think, and try. You made me feel appreciated, respected, needed, valuable, cared for, important, special, and supported.

You were always in my corner. Working for you has been one of the great pleasures of my life. Thank you, Ken, from the bottom of my heart. You gave me wings to fly.

No, Ken was not a teacher in the formal sense. But he taught me as much, if not more, than any formal teacher ever has. Ken taught me that I am one of a kind . . . and that it is nothing to be embarrassed about. Ken taught me to celebrate it and to soar with my strengths.

Why does anyone need to be taught?

Sometimes people have to learn the hard way. That is an old saying I have been hearing for years. It implies that there is an easy way too, although I have yet to enjoy that experience. I seem to have an innate ability to choose, if there really is a choice, to learn the hard way.

Writing this book was no exception. One would think the fact that I actually hired a writing coach with whom I would consult five days a week would signify an openness and willingness to learn . . . the easy way. No such luck. Oh, don't get me wrong. The desire was there. I earnestly wanted to learn. I was even willing to get out of bed every morning at four o'clock to practice the craft before going to my regular (paying) job. Sadly, even desire and diligence were not enough to prevent my frequent and seemingly involuntary resistance to follow my writing coach's advice.

It's an ironic situation, because I'm what you would call a lifelong learner, continuing my formal education throughout adulthood with both college credit programs and noncredit personal and professional development courses. I read to follow all the latest theories, and in the workplace I'm always pointing out the lesson in everyday events. I mentor young business associates to develop and hone their skills, and I even seek out my own mentors with whom I can interact to help clarify and validate my thinking.

Yet I frequently find that the most meaningful and life-enhancing lessons I learn are the hard ones . . . the ones against which I bend and bend and bend before I finally break and accept the learning. It's a phenomenon that is not so phenomenal. In fact, it's a characteristic we all share.

Thomas Kuhn called it paradigms. He wrote about it as a phenomena observed with scientists. When conducting experiments, their expectation for the results, based upon previous experiences and current assumptions, was powerful enough to literally cause them not to see results contrary to their expectations. The scientist's mind would automatically reject the unexpected results. Peter Senge referred to this as mental models that, in effect, form a barrier off of which anything new or different ricochets like a bouncing rubber ball.

It's nice to know that I'm in the company of brilliant scientists, but my paradigm muscle must be the strongest in my whole body.

"Why do I have to be so difficult?" I find myself repeatedly asking my writing coach. "Why don't I just keep my mouth shut and listen?" I ask him . . . for the tenth time.

Over and over again, I encounter these barriers to new ideas, new approaches, new constructs within which I need to work. This from someone who wants to learn! It must be exasperating for him.

"Don't think about it. Just do it!" he admonishes.

Often even his directness is unsuccessful to move me. I'm puzzled by my own behavior, still, I know in this I'm not alone.

As long ago as Plato's day, over three thousand years ago, he was writing about it, although the word paradigm had yet to be introduced. Those depicted in his *Allegory of the Cave* who clung desperately to their cave—to the only reality they had ever known— were exhibiting the same behavior I routinely exhibit. I know about paradigms—those mental models that place boundaries as impenetrable as those cave walls on our thinking. But, like the cave dwellers, I often seem powerless against it. It's a frustrating characteristic common to all humans. Yet it's not so uniquely human.

It's about security, the most basic need of all animals, human or otherwise. This quest for security first above all else is driven by what Weyant, Bernstein and Rozer refer to as our dinosaur brain. The dinosaur brain is the most prehistoric part of our being, the vestiges of an existence governed by survival of the fittest. Research has shown this survival instinct to be one of the primary functions of our left brain.

We have a tendency to refer to people as left-brained, if they are very analytical and logical, or right-brained, if they are highly creative and free-spirited. Yet the truth is we all have a dinosaur left brain that is constantly working to control our thoughts and actions in this blind pursuit of what appears to be logical and safe. My dinosaur brain seems to work overtime.

Tom Bird, noted author who writes about the process whereby we retrain our left brain to allow our right brain to lead, claims that the right brain is intended to lead. It's that creative, innovative, inventive side of us that *does* separate us from the rest of the animal kingdom. *Releasing the artist within* is what Tom calls it. *Releasing the human within* . . . the unique individual that each of us was born to be . . . that's what it means to me.

So I'm thankful for those hard lessons that jar the right brain until it's so wide awake that we don't even hear the dinosaur brain's roar, at least temporarily . . . at least long enough to release those flashes of brilliant enlightenment that sleep within each of us.

This is a real paradox. If the moments when our right brain is leading are so enjoyable and fulfilling, it begs the question even more. Why do we have to learn the hard way? Why are these satisfying moments so difficult to achieve?

Plato's allegory does not tell us how it was that the one cave dweller came to loosen his bonds. We just know that he did, and once he had experienced something new and better, his old paradigms were shattered. He learned from experience, which is how most of us do. After all, that's what learning the hard way is all about . . . learning from experience, albeit sometimes difficult or uncomfortable experiences, but learning that above all is dramatic enough to stick and to change our thoughts and actions from that point forward.

I've heard it said that some people hear the whisper of God, while others need to be hit with a brick. I believe that comment stems from this human characteristic. I also recognize that I frequently require the brick, but I doubt that I'm so unusual in that regard. The theory that people don't change until the pain of not changing becomes too great to bear seems to have risen from this fact of human nature.

Think about how an infant learns. Most babies learn very quickly that crying profusely brings about a desired response. Their primary caregivers will provide food, clean diapers, and cuddling. But compare that to orphaned babies. They learn just as quickly that crying doesn't improve their situation. There's no parent to rush to their aid and comfort. As a result, these babies rarely cry. They learn from experience that it serves no purpose. Experience is a great, although often hard, teacher. As children begin to mature—even orphaned children—they learn from experience. If they touch a hot stove, it will burn. If they run on a wet or icy surface, they will fall and get hurt. If they disobey, they will be punished. Once the pain becomes great enough, normally functioning children soon learn from experience to change their behavior. They learn the hard way.

I wish this were a process that stopped after adolescence. I wish I could have learned all those hard lessons in my youth and not have to continue to experience that painful growth in my adulthood. Such is not the case. It's a fact of life. We are all lifelong learners, whether we choose to refer to ourselves in that manner or not.

As long as my brain functions, I will continue to feel the need to tie a nice, secure little bow around my world. My dinosaur brain will continue to drive me subconsciously to create boundaries within which I will have a false sense of security and control. And I will continue to need those jarring, hard lessons that hit me with enough force to break through those mental boundaries . . . to escape the cave and free my spirit to soar . . . to stretch beyond my self-imposed limitations . . . to expand my sphere of existence . . . to be the person I was born to be.

I grew to know myself, due in part to the experience of working with Ken. Typically, our life-enhancing experiences occur through interaction with others. True, one can interact with God or nature, for instance, and experience life-changing revelations. Thoreau spent seven years on his Walden Pond experiencing his paradigm shifts. But most of us are not Thoreau, and even if we are close, it's difficult if not impossible in this day and age to find the solitude, separateness and serenity of Walden Pond. We have to find our Walden Pond in the hustle and bustle of today's world. We have to find our revelations in our interactions with other human beings. This has been true down through the ages, even in Thoreau's day. He was the exception, not the norm.

We learn from each other. Our learning is accelerated through interaction with others. That's what the enlightened cave dweller in Plato's allegory was trying to do for his imprisoned friends. He was attempting to accelerate their learning. He was trying to teach them, so they could enjoy the fruits of his enlightenment sooner rather than later . . . or possibly never.

We don't see this learning occur in Plato's *Allegory of the Cave*, because he was actually chronicling the rejection of Socrates, who was put to death over the misunderstanding of his attempts to help others learn and grow. The fact, however, of Socrates' life is that many did learn from him, Plato being one example. Socrates expanded the boundaries of some individual's thinking who might otherwise have taken much longer to learn, if at all. Socrates accelerated, enhanced, and enabled the learning of others. Yet he was just a man . . . an ordinary little man whose choice of lifestyle resulted in him being labeled a philosopher. But he was just a man . . . not particularly appealing physically nor was he charismatic. He was a man like any other we might meet on the street today . . . just like any other person through whom we are given equal opportunities to learn important lessons. Like the involuntary learning that a child experiences when they touch a hot stove, humans learn from and through one another. It is a fact of life.

Behavioral scientists and researchers Robert Carkhuff and Bernard Berenson state that all interactions are for better or worse. We will learn from all our interactions, good and bad. Just as the orphaned baby learns not to cry from the bad lesson of abandonment, the nurtured baby learns from the good lesson of love to cry out for attention. These lessons that continue throughout our lives as a direct result of all our good and bad interactions with one another are the necessary steps required to bring us closer and closer to becoming our one true self . . . that is, to be self-actualized. Each individual has a unique self to become, and therefore is driven by unique needs in that quest.

Thumbing through an old journal, I ran across a phrase I scribbled once, "Everyone I see is missing something." Now, years later, I reflect on that statement and wonder what it means. I think it's simply this. We're born by design incomplete creatures, which by default means we were created to learn and grow.

Regardless of your perspective, spiritual or scientific, evidence abounds that we're all wandering this earth . . . searching. For what are we searching? Ah, that's the question, isn't it? What will it take for us to feel satisfied? Money, material possessions, pleasurable activities, family, friends, rewarding career, meaningful pursuits, love, peace, happiness, joy . . . for what are we looking? Make no mistake, we are looking . . . all of us.

Count the number of avenues that now exist for that purpose . . . bars, nightclubs, concerts, churches, continuing education, career planning and placement services, Web sites, television, radio, financial planning services, plays, musicals, street fairs, golf clubs, yacht clubs, hiking clubs, singles clubs . . . the list goes on and on and on. The paths down which an individual's search for satisfaction may lead seem countless and yet still growing.

What drives us as human beings to wander down so many roads? Do we really believe that we know ourselves completely and know exactly what we want and how to get it? Or do we hope that eventually we will reach "the end" of the journey and wander into our one true self waiting there to be discovered?

Someone asked me this question once point blank. "What drives you? Why are you never satisfied?"

The question shocked me because it came from someone who knew me pretty well, who had known me for a good ten years. Do I seem so abnormal? I wondered. She didn't mean it to be flattering and looked at me as though I was some kind of alien. I was stunned, both by the question as well as the attitude with which she posed it. But even more disturbing was the fact that I didn't know the answer. What does drive me? What is it that drives all of us?

We are created with a pleasure response in our body chemistry. Hormones and other chemicals exist in our physical makeup for the sheer purpose of providing a pleasurable physiological response to various stimuli. All human beings share that characteristic. And yet each individual is slightly different, requiring a unique set of specific stimuli to achieve that pleasure response. For some it is family, a nice home, a few vacations throughout the year and financial security. For others it may be artistic, cultural pursuits allowing them to create through such venues as writing, music, drama, painting, or sculpting. Perhaps it involves more natural stimuli like those found in hiking, camping, rafting, boating, horse-back riding, or rock climbing. And then there are the more extreme methods with new ones springing up every day, some even perceived to border on obsessive or immoral behavior, but all still sharing the same common denominator . . . the drive, inexplicable though it may be, of the individual to satisfy his or her need for pleasure.

Does that sound shallow to you? There was a song on the radio recently containing a line that stuck in my head about whether life really is just about the next great fad. Are we really such self-absorbed, pleasure-seeking creatures? Surely the number of people who have devoted serious amounts of time—even their lives—to charitable, volunteer or nonprofit, helping endeavors is evidence to the contrary. But think about it. Why do we engage in charitable activities? Why do we give our time and money to those less fortunate than ourselves? The answer is because we want to help people, right? Well, yes, that's true. But it goes deeper than that. I want to help others because of how it makes me feel. I feel better. I get that chemical pleasure response. I do it for me.

In preparation for a mission trip to an orphanage in Guatemala, home to five hundred orphans of all ages from newborns to college age, I began the medical precautions necessary when being exposed to the living conditions of a Third-World country. In so doing, I found myself talking to the lab worker who was drawing my blood in the doctor's office. She had been on two previous short-term mission trips, like the one I was about to take, and was preparing to return again with a medical team to Costa Rica.

She smiled at me as she spoke from experience. "You will get so much out of this. It will change your life." A glow appeared on her face as she continued. "You know, you think you're going to help them. But you're really going for yourself. Don't get me wrong. They will benefit from you being there. But you will get so much more out of it than they will."

She was right. Now I'm convinced that everything we do, even the most charitable of acts, is driven by our desire to feel pleasure . . . to have those peak experiences . . . to feel good about ourselves and our human experience.

So that's the ultimate answer to the question that stumped me years ago. "What drives you?" she'd asked, and then added, "Sometimes there isn't a reason. Some things just are."

At the time, I agonized over it. Assuming that being continually driven was some sort of criminal indictment, I'd searched for all the wrongs perpetrated on me in childhood and young adulthood that had turned me into such a terrible, driven person . . . parents, clergy, teachers, and authority figures, society. The source, the reason, the root cause of the *problem* was *out there* . . . external to me . . . impersonal.

Now, finally, I can take exception to her assertion. There is a reason. There is a reason for it all. And I realize the answer to her question is not out there. The answer is inside me. The answer is inside all of us. The answer is, I am driven by the same thing that drives each of us. Even more importantly, it is not a problem at all. It is the most natural thing in human nature. We are all searching down our own unique path to find that which pleasures us most . . . that part of us that is missing . . . the fulfillment of our own unique potential . . . the *reason* we are here.

The feeling and fulfillment of desires is a natural part of our progression toward being all that we can be. Self-actualization is "the desire to become more and more what one is, to become everything one is capable of becoming." It is independent of culture and environment. Regardless of one's environment, the individual will still be driven by the desires that lead to self-realization.

Maslow illustrated his theory in the following manner. "Musicians must make music, artists must paint, poets must write, if they are to be ultimately at peace with themselves. What humans *can* be, they *must* be."

It's that undeniable drive within to fulfill our own unique purpose—common to all of mankind—that makes us all students. Whether we are conscious of the source of our desires . . . whether we are intentional about our journey . . . whether we are focused on our growth or just accepting temporary, pleasurable substitutes . . . even if we are just learning in a careless, haphazard manner . . . we are nevertheless learning creatures driven by our own unfulfilled purpose. We are all students. And, because our learning is accelerated by our interaction with one another, we also are teachers. We are, at once, both. Oh, how enriched our journey here together would be if only we worked at being the best possible students and teachers we can be!

What is a teacher?

How do we do that? How can we all be teachers? In an unexpected way, I was recently confronted with that question. As an alumna of the Master of Arts in adult education program at a local college, I had been asked to facilitate a focus group made up of current students. The intent had been to gather feedback for the purpose of improving all aspects of the program, including the content, environment, teachers, and group dynamics. Suddenly, halfway into the meeting, one of the adult student's comments cut with a razor-sharp edge through the fluff to the heart of the matter.

He looked at me with pleading eyes. "I enrolled in this Master's program because I wanted to learn how to teach. Now I'm two-thirds finished, and I still don't know how. I need someone to teach me how to be a teacher!"

His words struck a chord deep inside me. They were about to become degreed educators of adults yet did not think they knew how to teach.

Comments like those make teaching and learning sound so mystical, yet in all parts of the civilized and uncivilized world, humans become students from birth. We are constantly learning, exposed to teachers both formal and informal, who teach many important life lessons. Beyond this natural learning process, some people pursue teaching as a profession, these students being prime examples. To these individuals, being a teacher means being their one true self.

And, since we are continually learning our way to becoming the person we were born to be, it's clear that we need these formal teachers who are dedicated to breaking our old paradigms. No wonder this student seemed intimidated. Teachers accomplish feats that sometimes seem Herculean. It must have felt to my childhood teachers as if it would take the strength of Hercules to lift me and my classmates from our myopic existence. It wasn't because we were from the country. We could have been anywhere. Instead it was because of our limited sphere of existence. We could have had a limited, inner-city sphere of existence or a limited, country-club sphere. These little microcosms in which we live become caves, keeping the outside world at bay, and ours was no different. I needed teachers to help me become aware of what I didn't know I didn't know . . . of what was outside my current sphere.

Everyone experiences this same phenomenon. The pie of all there is to know contains three slices for everyone: what we know we know, what we know we don't know, and what we don't know we don't know. Everyone's pie has those three slices with the size of the three essentially the same in everyone's pie. What varies is the content of each slice. The contents of the three slices are unique to each and every individual. As an individual, we can never know all there is to know, that is, the whole pie. But an individual can have something in his or her known slice that exists in another's unknown slice. Facilitating the sharing of that knowledge is what a formal teacher does. A person functioning in a formal teacher role can plan activities and hand out assignments that prompt individuals to research and learn from someone who knows something they, themselves, do not. Whether the learning is from the author of a book, some notable leader, the teacher, or even the student sitting across the aisle in class, teachers facilitate awareness of *what we don't know we don't know.*

In less formal ways, we all can present this same learning and awareness challenge to one another. Therefore, at one time or another, we are all teaching. We may be doing it consciously as a formal teacher, as a parent, or as a manager. We may be doing it unconsciously as a friend, as a fellow student, as a co-worker, or as an innocent bystander. Make no mistake, we are all teaching.

The answer to the question, "What is a teacher?" begins with the realization that we are all always teaching someone something—maybe good, maybe bad—but teaching something nonetheless. We can prove this further by listening to the comments of any formal teacher. "I can't do it all." They will agree. "It has to start in the home." That was clearly the case for me growing up. I had already learned much before going to school or reaching an age at which I was more aware. Whether my parents and the other folks who made up my small world realized it or not, they were teaching me volumes every day.

Since we are all teaching all the time maybe the more important question is not simply "What is a teacher?" but rather "What makes one a *good* teacher?" After all, like the old saying goes, you can lead a horse to water, but you can't make him drink.

To understand what makes one a good teacher, let's begin by looking at what a student is. It stands to reason that if I can be teaching others, consciously or unconsciously, from time to time, then I'm also learning from others, consciously or unconsciously. One time I may be the person who leads the horse to water, and the next time I may be the horse.

Growing up on a farm, I had lots of experience with the origins of this old proverb. Riding my horse through the fields on a hot summer day was one of my few pleasures, and, occasionally, I would stop thinking about my own enjoyment long enough to worry about my trusty steed. She must be thirsty, I would think, and we're still a long way from the barn. This may be our last opportunity for water, I'd realize, as I dismounted and led her down to the creek. And then she would do it. Amazing though it may seem, on that hot, dry, summer day, when she was being forced to tote me around through the pastures and the woods, she would balk. There before her ran cold, clear water. "You must be thirsty!" I'd say, admonishing her and tugging on the reins to urge her toward the water. "Don't pass up this opportunity!" I would add, to no avail. Against all logic, she'd stand there staring at me and not drink a drop. You can lead a horse to water, but you can't make her drink.

When we're acting as a teacher, we are exposing others to what they don't know they don't know. We're leading them to the water. When we're acting as student, like the horse, we choose whether we will drink. Students exercise free will. As a student, it is a choice we make, either knowingly or blindly, to be open and allow ourselves to learn or to be closed or inattentive or antagonistic and learn nothing.

This brings us right back to the original question. As a student, why do we have to learn the really good lessons the hard way? Why do we not just drink the water freely? Carl Jung says that our greatest growth comes out of pain. It is during those survive-or-die periods in our lives when our mental models are shaken enough to make us more open to the spirit within that's trying to lead us to fulfillment of self . . . fulfillment of purpose. So, as a student, periods of pain, uncertainty, and change are our friends. Without those hard lessons our dinosaur brain would lead us to settle for a limiting sense of identity.

That's what happened to me. By the time I reached forty, I had pretty much pigeon-holed myself. My sense of identity was all bound up in my experiences up to that point in my life. I saw myself as a reasonably successful businesswoman, both blessed and cursed with a hardworking, independent streak born out of my country and farm origins. The people I grew up with were farmers or blue-collar workers or both, and although I'd managed to rise to a white-collar job, in my head that's what I was too. That was my sense of identity. Anything outside of that was rejected.

Even when the desire to write . . . that unfulfilled purpose inside . . . started tugging at my heart, my hardened sense of identity fought against it. I began reading the literary works of all the great masters, apparently in an attempt to convince myself once and for all that I couldn't write. I certainly couldn't write like *that*, I told myself. For a long time, it worked. My dinosaur brain won the battle. "Don't take that risk," it said to me. "It might not be safe. You might fail. Stick with what you know."

The sad truth is that what happened with me is not unusual. We all get wrapped up in a sense of identity that will exclude other possibilities. My writing coach, Tom Bird, says it's not that we're afraid of failure, but that we're afraid of success. If I am a writer, what does that do to my sense of identity? It doesn't fit into that neat little package I've spent forty years creating.

What's worse, the people who share my current sphere of existence only know the person who is the hardworking businesswoman. A writer? They either look at me like I've grown a second head or as though they feel sorry for me. "Bless her heart, she's going through her midlife crisis," their condescending and pitying looks seem to say. If it's a midlife phenomenon, so be it. Thankfully, it happened eventually.

Henry David Thoreau said, "If one advances confidently in the direction of their dreams and lives the life that they've imagined, they will meet with success unexpected in common hours." I don't know if that's what I did, or if it was more like succumbing to

What lies behind us and what lies before us are tiny matters compared to what lies within us.
–Ralph Waldo Emerson

an inevitable destiny. What is a midlife crisis anyway? It seems to be the time in people's lives when they go on a dream vacation, buy a dream car . . . boat . . . house (insert your favorite poison), have an affair, or worse yet, divorce their spouse of umpteen years. Those are the symptoms, anyway. But what's the cause? What drives people to such great lengths at such predictable times in their lives?

The reason we all know what the phrase "midlife crisis" means is because of the simple fact that we're all driven by the same basic urge, the same core need, to live the one true life that we were born to live. We reach middle age and see the last remaining vestiges of our youth slipping away. It's then, whether we realize it or not, that we're driven to finally know . . . before we die . . . why we're alive. In this context, the midlife crisis isn't a crisis at all. Rather, it's an awakening. The midlife awakening does not need to be a crisis. It's only the misguided urges we give in to that can make it a time of crisis in which we destroy relationships, finances, lives, homes, and reputations. If we instead recognize it for what it truly is—an awakening—an awareness to the reason we're here and the purpose we were born to fulfill, then it can be a time of celebration.

"I didn't have a midlife crisis," I've heard some people say. This always makes me think, in that case, I'm either very happy for you or very, very sad. Happy, if that means you knew from an extremely young age exactly why you're here and have moved purposefully in that direction daily. Extremely sad, if that means that you have just moved mindlessly and blindly through day after routine day and never once stopped to wonder, dream, imagine, or reflect on a unique purpose . . . never even allowed yourself to consider it, as though that would somehow be a bad thing.

I met a young man one time who was an artist. He was a quiet, gentle, thoughtful, sensual, creative creature and struck me as someone who was most certainly following his heart, letting his right brain lead, moving confidently in the direction of the life his spirit was leading him toward. This pleased and intrigued me, so I asked him, "Tell me what you dream about."

"What?" He looked at me in bewilderment.

"What you dream about," I continued. "When you imagine yourself doing anything in the world and feeling totally and completely happy and satisfied, what is the life that you dream of?"

He was struck dumb. "I don't know." He finally muttered in confusion.

How could this be, I wondered, that such a young, artistic person so obviously connected with his inner, creative spirit was apparently not at all aware of the source of his urges, had never thought beyond the current expression of those urges, and had never dreamed of where they might lead? In fact, the more I got to know him, the more I realized how hard he was trying to live a *normal* life, how eager he was to jump into the rat race and live the American dream.

He had the graphic artist job at a large corporation. He had the beautiful, young, blonde girlfriend, the starter home in the nice neighborhood, and the dog to lead them on morning walks through it. He was already on the same cookie-cutter path that we all scramble to jump on, ASAP! Just like I did when I went to work at nineteen, married at twenty-one, and built a house at twenty-two. By twenty-three years of age, I was so deeply in debt and problems, trying to work, survive a bad marriage, and still finish school, I didn't know what I was doing. I was so confused. I didn't even realize that I wasn't living my dream. I was only doing the same thing everyone else was doing. That seemed to make it right.

Redfield writes about this phenomenon of human existence. We so quickly become conditioned to the prevailing culture—losing connection with the source of our being amidst the noise and distractions in the world around us—that we are letting others decide for us before we ever, even, realize it. We are not moving confidently in the direction of the life we have dreamed about. We are not dreaming at all, but simply playing a sad game of follow the leader. What's worse is this blind amble leads us to our governing sense of identity.

Our sense of identity . . . who we think we are . . . our perception of ourselves often is based upon the role we play in other's lives. I am mother, father, big brother, or little sister. I am nurse, protector, provider, companion, or caretaker. Sometimes we derive our identity from what we do for a living. I am an accountant, a manager, a secretary, a customer service rep, a teacher, a farmer, a welder, a truck driver, a salesman, or a retiree. The list goes on and on. We look to every possible external source for our identity. In addition, we also turn to marital status, sexual orientation, social class, income level, education level or type, religious affiliation, hobbies, talents, possessions . . . we heap one descriptor on top of another in an attempt to answer the simple question, "Who am I, and why am I here?" But most, if not all, of these fail to truly answer the question. They are mere symbols of the path (or rut) into which we have blindly fallen. It reminds me of a sign I heard was posted on the westward wagon trail. "Avoid this rut or you will be stuck in it for the next 25 miles."

By midlife, if not sooner, something happens to cause most people to realize they need more of a balance. This awakening for me was gradual. The pain of a failed marriage, coupled with nagging desires to go down a different path, gradually forced me to challenge my current sense of identity. The whole process finally culminated at age forty, when I realized my life was half over. I realized I still have much to do, so I'd better get moving. I needed to climb out of the rut and make some forward progress.

Now I was really going to be a good student. I had conquered that old limiting sense of identity . . . or so I thought. True, I had actually shocked people with the proclamation that I was going to be a writer. I had even gone to classes, hired a coach, and started a book. But the dinosaur brain is relentless.

"Okay, okay, you're a writer," it reluctantly conceded. "But you're a certain kind of writer. You're a good short story writer. You can tell other people's story. Yeah, yeah, I know you think you have important messages for other people, but you need to disguise those messages in your sweet little stories. Who would want to hear what you think anyway?"

My left brain was safely back in control. It was so subtle and natural; I didn't even know it happened. I thought I was being an excellent student. Following Tom's guidance, I tore through production of the first manuscript. I was writing! I was happy. Life was great! I fired off the manuscript to Tom for review, composed of eight loosely linked short stories through which I hoped the reader would get the point.

"You've done well," my left brain told me. "You've produced a good, safe little book. Now we know who you are again."

Tom's reaction was mixed. "What you've written is fine, but where are you? You're not there. You only show up briefly and tentatively at the very end. You need to be present right from the beginning and throughout the book."

What in the world is he talking about? I wondered. Of course I'm present. I wrote it. I've done exactly what I meant to do. This is the kind of writer I am, I reasoned.

Never mind that it was my first attempt to write a book. I was convinced that I knew better than anyone, better than him certainly, what kind of writer I am.

"This is what I write!" I complained to my sister . . . my true supporter.

"Yes," she agreed, "That's what you're good at, those short essays in which you take a real-life event and weave it into a story that can make people laugh, cry, and learn all at once," she affirmed.

Never mind that this was simply the only kind of writing I'd ever attempted, and thus the only product of mine she'd ever read. Never mind that I'd hired Tom to teach me how to do more. Never mind that I'd intended to be a good student. My rejection of his attempts to teach me was immediate and subconscious and powerful.

It's ironic that I would fall victim to this so easily, when I've made a career out of leading groups to avoid this very behavior. As a trained facilitator, one of the things we try to help people do is avoid placing limits on a situation. Especially when facilitating brainstorming activities, the intent is to totally open up the realm of possibility, so that one person can feed off the ideas of another. Yet time and time again, what I've seen is how quickly a person will identify with his or her own idea. Sometimes it is a pet project or a hidden agenda they've been harboring for years, and they're trying to use this activity as a way to recycle it and gain support for it again. So they're prepared to fight for it against all alternatives.

But even more frequent is the situation in which a person has no preconceived notions and has an idea pop into their head literally only seconds before they articulate it to the group. Then even though the idea only just occurred to them, they begin to defend it vigorously. No matter how hard the facilitator tries to allow the process to continue, to enable this latest idea to be another block on which new ideas can continue to be built, you can see the wheels turning in the head of the person who came up with it. Sometimes they'll withdraw from the process totally, either because they are lost in their own world thinking further about their own idea or because they feel so rejected by the lack of total acceptance for it. Sometimes, rather than withdrawing, they become more vocal, almost fighting, to convince the group that their idea is the answer for which the group is searching. Maybe it is. But unless the process is allowed to continue, we can't know that for sure. It's a process I know well.

Yet here I was, defending my manuscript to Tom. I exhibited all those behaviors. I argued for my approach and structure. I went out and enlisted reinforcements to back me up in my assertion. When that didn't cause Tom to concede, I took the other course of action. I withdrew. I dropped out of the process altogether. I couldn't accept any other approach. This had to be it. I had no ideas . . . no words. My creativity shut down. I was totally blocked. My new, fragile sense of identity was on shaky ground, and my dinosaur brain had kicked into high gear. I was fighting for survival, yes, but with all the wrong ammunition.

Tom's persistence made the difference. His diligence to be a teacher, whether I wanted to be a student anymore or not, kept the door from going completely closed. "He's going to keep calling you every day whether or not you ever attempt what he's asking you to do," my logical left brain finally admitted. "The only way you're ever going to get any peace is to at least try."

So one Saturday morning I gave in. I let go of my brief identity as a short story writer. I started to write again and, to my surprise, the words gushed out. A few short weeks earlier I'd been utterly convinced that I knew who I was. I knew what I was doing. I was sure I had absolutely exhausted every word that I had to write on this subject. And I was absolutely wrong. Even though my newfound sense of identity as a short story writer was better than the old nonwriter identity it had replaced, it had quickly established new limits. It's an unfortunate reality we all face. It's why being a good student is so important and so difficult all at the same time.

Mind you, a clear sense of identity is not a bad thing. It's an important part of being a healthy human being. Successful development of a clear sense of identity is crucial to our mental health and fulfillment. The trick is in how we choose to identify ourselves.

You heard me correctly. Even something like our identity, which may seem predestined, is a choice we make. Even if certain inclinations are predestined, I can still choose whether or not I act on the desires of my heart. Choice has such a monumental impact on the quality of our lives. This is true due to the link between choice and accountability, a universal principle of our human existence. The explanation of that assertion lies first in understanding what a principle is.

Principles are inarguable truths. Principles of science are the easiest to understand. Gravity, for instance, is a principle of science. I could argue, albeit foolishly, that gravity does not exist. Nevertheless, if I jumped from the roof, I would stand (or should I say fall) corrected. Gravity would still operate, whether I believed in it or not. That is what principles do. They operate whether we realize it and take advantage of that reality or not. Astronauts, aviators, and engineers of all types know how the principle of gravity works, and they use it to achieve positive results. My ignorance or denial of this principle in my jumping from the roof example yields negative results.

Such is the case with all these universal principles of human existence. When I understand and operate in accordance with these principles, I can generate positive, natural consequences. Likewise, if I do not, I will generate negative, natural consequences. Principles operate in my world, and how I interact with them generates a continual stream of positive and negative consequences in my life. Simple as that.

This gravity example is pretty easy to understand. But how can we say that choice and accountability are also universal principles of human existence? Think about it. Humans make choices all the time. As soon as we begin to develop even the tiniest sense of awareness, we begin to choose how we will act or think and how we will feel or respond to the stimuli around us. By the time we hit the "terrible twos," even as toddlers, we are fighting desperately to make choices, and there are always consequences. Being deprived of our free will is probably the most miserable of existences. It's why we use incarceration to punish those who break the law; that is, those who have chosen not to operate in accordance with the universal principles of existence, thus generating negative consequences. Choice and accountability are principles that operate, whether we are conscious of the number of choices we make, and whether we are aware of the consequences our choices are generating. Consider this example.

Imagine a scenario where you are driving down the interstate lost in reflection about your day at work. It was an especially difficult day filled with unexpected interruptions, unreasonable demands, unclear expectations and one crisis after another. You're working all the overtime you can, but still all hopes of receiving a promotion seem out the window. You really need that salary increase now that both kids are driving and starting to college. You're dreading the prospect of taking out a second mortgage on the house, when you can barely handle the first one. How could your spouse not understand why you are tired and grumpy all the time? Who wouldn't be? You grow angry as you drive because of the realization that no one understands the pressure you are under.

Then out of nowhere a driver, maneuvering erratically, cuts you off! He almost hit you! You had to slam on your brakes to let him in, causing the 18-wheeler behind you to narrowly miss your back bumper as he swerved into the emergency lane while blaring his loud horn in your ear. You floor the accelerator again and, without fully realizing what you're doing, in an instant you are in pursuit of the crazy driver who caused the situation, blasting your horn in return. When you get close enough to see his eyes in the rear view mirror, he gives you the old one-finger salute, slips into another gear, and rips down the highway. You become enraged like never before. This is the last straw! You will not allow another person to disrespect you. You speed after the other car, maneuvering carelessly through traffic, swerving erratically from one lane to another. You have one singular mission in mind when, suddenly, your concentration is shattered by a familiar sight and sound . . . blue lights and a state trooper siren.

Of course, it was the other driver's fault, you explain. He *caused* it. He *made* you do what you did. As the trooper continues to write your citation, the message is clear. No, you had a choice. You chose to behave in the manner you did. Now you are accountable for the result of that choice. An effective person—one who is aware of how the principles of choice and accountability operate—recognizes that they have options, such as not chasing after the careless, rude driver on the highway.

Heraclites, a Greek philosopher who lived between 540–480 BC, wrote that although we humans do not always think alike or have the same degree of reason, there must be a kind of universal reason (those principles of existence) guiding everything that happens in nature. Yet he observed that most people try to live by their own individual reason. People want to conveniently forget about the principle of accountability. God and society may not hold us accountable for the results of our actions until a certain chronological age, but we see these principles of choice and accountability operating upon all people of all ages in the world. People of all ages make choices, and then they experience the consequences. They are accountable for the results of those choices.

With this in mind, being a good student and avoiding a narrow sense of identity that limits the possibilities for learning and growth involves being aware of choice and accountability. To be a good student, you need to realize that you are able to choose your identity. Moreover, you must choose carefully, because your choices will have consequences. Your choice will open some doors and close others. So you must make choices thoughtfully and intently, not haphazardly or carelessly. Furthermore, you must continually examine the results you are generating. Is it really what you wanted? What choices resulted in your current state? What new choices can you make? What new ways can you evolve your sense of identity to generate increasingly desirable results? Remember, even doing nothing is in itself a choice. Being a good student means making the choice to learn and apply the things that consistently challenge your paradigms and enhance your sense of identity—an identity that you are actively managing and developing throughout your human existence.

Your life is not a coincidence. It's a reflection of you! – Author Unknown

Okay. If that's what makes one a good student, then what makes one a good teacher? Let us not forget that we are all students and teachers at one time or another. A good teacher, then, understands what it feels like to be a student. A good teacher understands that students are unique individuals making a journey . . . striving deliberately or driven carelessly to fulfill their purpose . . . their reason for being here. They may be struggling to maintain a healthy sense of identity and continued psychosocial development, or they may have simply given up the struggle altogether. They will certainly be dealing with their own paradigms, resisting change and fearing the unknown . . . fearing the success that will challenge their safe sense of identity. Students will be making choices and operating either with or against the principles of human existence and dealing with the negative consequences they generate. And they will be carrying around all sorts of unresolved issues stemming from these uniquely human struggles. Students will be dealing with one or more of these things or all the above.

A good teacher knows and understands this—has compassion and empathy for it—because a teacher is also a flawed, struggling student. A good teacher has no illusions to the contrary about themselves. A good teacher is mindful of his or her student's struggles and supports them. A good teacher does not judge students harshly for resistance to learn, change, and grow. A good teacher understands, because they have been there . . . they are there. A good teacher does not allow the frustration of student resistance or rejection to deter them. A good teacher does not stop teaching.

That is what Tom did with me. He kept right on teaching, even when I didn't appear to want to learn anymore. He knew what I was going through. He held the mirror up in front of me and made me aware of it too. He didn't give up on me. A *good* teacher, like a *good* student, never gives up.

Tom says that one of the greatest tragedies is that some people may never live the life they were born to live. Jung's and Redfield's theories make it sound as though fulfillment of self—or at least at a minimum the midlife realization of a more balanced perception of self—is inevitable. But it isn't inevitable. What is inevitable, however, is feeling the continual pull, the inexplicable drive, that tugs relentlessly . . . the need that we attempt to satisfy in so many different ways.

As teachers we must remember that each aspect of every interaction with others teaches them something on their journey. In my case, when I began to tell people I was going to write, their condescending looks were teaching me that I should doubt myself . . . not a lesson from which I could benefit at that fragile stage of the journey.

We're always both student and teacher. Fulfilling the purpose for which we were born is too important to be left to chance. We must all nurture one another in this joint endeavor. And that's what a good teacher does.

A teacher, formal or informal, offers the student a choice. The student will, hopefully, choose with the realization that any choice will have either positive or negative natural consequences. These results will teach further lessons, either good or bad, whether conscious or subconscious. The point is it all starts with a choice. Students choose. Students exercise free will. If I'm your student, or your child, or your employee, your friend, your patient, whatever, if I'm playing the role of student with you acting even temporarily as my teacher, don't forget that I will choose what I learn or whether I learn anything at all.

Students are free-will creatures blocked and bound up by all sorts of barriers and hurdles, who choose what they learn and who they learn it from. This makes it easy to see that the way to be a good teacher is to be adept at leading them to choose to learn more often . . . to motivate them to make more choices with positive natural consequences. A good teacher is one who can cause the student to open up . . . to become more aware of what they don't know . . . to see the water . . . and to want to drink it. A good teacher recognizes that you can't make students drink. A good teacher does not push or demand. A good teacher leads and inspires.

Why do teachers and students need each other?

Now we know why we need to be taught, what it is to be a good student, and how to be a good teacher. Beyond that we need to recognize why teachers and students need one another . . . why we humans need to engage in these teacher-student behaviors together in order to be all that we were born to be.

We've examined how becoming the person we were born to be is a lifelong process. We must learn from all our good and bad interactions the lessons crucial to that continual development. Along the way, we must recognize that the enculturation process in society trains our left brain to lead . . . to create a governing sense of identity. We must fight against this stagnation, allow our right brain to lead, and consciously make the choices that will bring us ever closer to our one true self. To experience the joy of enlightened existence . . . the joy we are meant to know in this life . . . to have those peak experiences one after another, we must diligently challenge the paradigms and stretch the boundaries that are formed by our left brain in the misguided aim of protecting us. We must be awakened to what drives us and embrace it . . . allow it to lead. There's a quote from an unknown source that expresses what our approach in this life should be.

> *Life should not be a journey to the grave with the intention of arriving safely in a pretty and well-preserved body, but rather to skid in broadside, thoroughly used up, totally worn out, and loudly shouting, "Wow, what a ride!"*

So how do we do that, and why does it sometimes seem so difficult? James Redfield, in *The Celestine Vision*, describes the universe as a dynamic system characterized by a constant flow of miracles creating a platform for us to fulfill our deepest and most heartfelt aspirations. This description makes the whole idea of self-actualization seem simple, even inevitable. Nevertheless, as Tom Bird points out, many people will still die without living the life they were meant to live.

Redfield explains that this is due to many factors. We get lost in the noise and confusion of the world. We lose touch with our own inner voice . . . our spirit . . . lose the connection with the source. Weakened by this, we begin to engage in control dramas to try to steal energy from others. We feel temporarily pumped up if we can best, show up, put down, or control someone else. Soon, however, this temporary high wears off, sending us in search of our next conquest. We don't even realize we are doing it. We don't recognize the voice inside attempting to guide us toward the right choices. We're still trying to get where we feel driven to go. Sometimes we even feel like we might be so close to being on the right track. But we sure could use a little help getting over the hump. We need those teachers who have a different perspective than we do . . . those who have the vision to see what could be, even when we ourselves can't see it. That's what helps us over the hump.

In the tale of the emperor's new clothes, we find a relevant metaphor. The emperor was tricked by those he trusted into believing he was elegantly clothed, even though he was naked. Then because he was the emperor, no one dared to challenge him and make him aware of the truth about himself. Likewise, we are deceived by others' view of who we are. As we mature, we gradually become the person our parents and elders teach us to be. We put on the clothes they give us. Soon we're active participants in our own deception, accepting this façade, wearing this identity proudly like a new suit. But, like the emperor, we have blind spots. We're blind, not only to our weaknesses, but also to many of our strengths.

Jung describes how these truths lurk in the shadow of our unconscious mind. Our unconsciousness, whether personal or collective to our species, contains all that we are and all that we have ever experienced. These suppressed memories, which may be good or bad, are packed away either to be recalled one day when the need arises or to never be thought of consciously again.

Within our unconscious mind is our shadow, containing all that, for whatever reason, we have disowned. Even a part of the purpose we were born to fulfill can end up buried in the dumping ground of our shadow. Here's how that happens. If I was born with the urge to be a writer, but was raised in a family and environment that instead valued more physical, labor-intensive, blue-collar pursuits, I will most likely have buried my artistic writer's expression in my shadow. We may find treasures such as this lurking in the shadow of our unconscious mind, but it's a murky mess in there with barriers constructed at every turn to keep the contents hidden.

That's why we need teachers. We need help navigating through the self-imposed barriers and around the inhibitors to find the capabilities, strengths and possibilities hidden in our psyche. Because we have our unconsciousness, our blind spots, our weaknesses and our shadow, we don't always see a clear picture of ourselves. Like the emperor with no clothes, we need someone to hold up a mirror to reveal the truth to us.

Consider these situations. Have you ever thought there was something wrong with your lawn tractor and called a repairman, only to learn that it was simply out of gas? What about this? Have you ever had a problem with a piece of electronic equipment and called a customer service hotline for assistance? What is the first question they ask? "Have you confirmed that the device is connected to a power source?" They ask you if it's plugged in. Duh! But you'd be surprised how many times this is actually the problem. It's so obvious that it's overlooked. It is not visible in our current perspective. We're so convinced that we're on the right track, the answer is virtually invisible to us. The customer service representative helps us see things we can't see. That's why we need teachers. That's why we all must be good teachers. It's a customer service mentality to humanity. It's about helping others find their answers in their unconscious mind . . . to make their unconsciousness conscious.

We can replace the earlier pie analogy, which represented all that could be known, with this analogy of the cup. Our conscious mind is like a full teacup. If we try to pour more into it when it's already full, the contents would just spill over and end up wasted on the floor. By expanding the boundaries of our consciousness, a good teacher, in effect, gives us a larger cup . . . a larger space within which to cultivate a new, more liberating sense of identity. Then like a good customer service rep, a person acting as teacher in a given situation facilitates the process of sorting out the contents inside and outside our cup of consciousness and helps us decide what combination will work best for us. Teachers help us make good choices that bring us into the light of awareness and ever closer to the person we are driven to be.

This theory holds even if I believe that I'm created with a preordained purpose by a supreme being. Proverbs 27:17 in the Bible states, "As iron sharpens iron, so one man sharpens another." We need help from one another . . . we need teachers . . . even to fulfill a divinely inspired purpose. Rick Warren, pastor, author of *The Purpose Driven Life*, and a leading proponent of the concept of a Godly purpose, is himself a teacher. Even those who share his belief that we have a divine purpose, which God can reveal to us, needed Warren to write that book and develop the self-study and training program that supplements it. Regardless of your perspective, religious or secular, we all need teachers.

The average life span of humans is 25,550 days. I find myself surprised by how short that seems. I want thousands more days than that. But I won't have them. And each one is too important to waste. What we do with them in pursuit of a fulfilled purpose in this life is too valuable to be left to chance. We all need good teachers who help us make the most of each precious second.

So that's why we as students need teachers. But what does teaching do for us when we teach? Why do teachers need students?

I had a teacher in school who apparently thought it was just to have a steady paycheck. A curmudgeonly old man, he told us about how he left the farm in his youth to go north to work in the auto factories that drew many from the south in those days. Soon, however, he found himself homesick and looking for a job that could support him and his growing family into his retirement years in the southern hometown he loved.

Surveying the job landscape, he had concluded there would always be kids and public schools they were required to attend, so teaching would be a stable job.

That blue-collar mentality totally infused his teaching style and was evident in everything he did. He approached each day like the factory worker who feels he is just getting paid for showing up for his appointed eight hours a day. This man had no plan to teach at all. He made us take turns reading a paragraph from the book, one student after another, around and around the room we went until the class period was over. The only variation was that sometimes we started on the left side of the room instead of the right.

> The great aim of education is not knowledge but action.
> – Herbert Spencer

It was a numbing process that routinely put teacher and students alike to sleep in the early morning eight o'clock class. He barely even knew our names. He certainly didn't know me. I eventually graduated as covaledictorian of my class with a straight A grade point average . . . despite him, I might add.

When he distributed grade reports after our first six weeks, I was mortified to see a D on my report card. "This man is out of his mind!" I thought. I'd never missed a class and never missed a single question on the simplistic fill-in-the-blank tests he had lifted straight from the text we blandly read aloud each morning. And he certainly couldn't deduct points for lack of class participation. I participated as much as anyone could. I read my appointed paragraphs. So I gathered up all my old tests, approached him and challenged the grade, and he changed it to an A.

It was all mindless and meaningless to him. He certainly was not getting anything out of the experience—neither were we—and he missed a fleeting opportunity to know us, his students, as the unique individuals we were. This man did *not* live the life of the enlightened teacher we deserved at that time in our lives . . . the kind of teacher we all deserve to encounter over and over in our lives. To him, we were just a paycheck.

He is the poster child for why this book is needed. The world needs for us all to be good teachers . . . aware of the impact—good or bad—we are having on each other's development at all times.

And here's the good news. If we become that enlightened, engaged teacher that the world and the students in it so desperately need, our own lives will be enriched beyond our wildest imagination . . . far beyond the few pieces of silver that he was so keen on being paid for the service.

Edwin Markham wrote, "There is a destiny that makes us all brothers. None goes his way alone. All that we send into the lives of others comes back into our own."

Quantum physicists might reword this to say, there is an energy that makes us all connected. Whether you believe as Einstein did that atoms are as real as this book you are holding in your hand, or if you believe like his opponents that atoms are not visible but rather tiny packets of energy—complex beyond our capacity to understand or visualize— both schools of thought agree there exists a complicated web of relations between all energy particles that comprise all forms of matter. This web of energy relationships—a quantum field of energy—below the surface of all things in the world establishes interconnectedness. We are all connected, one to another, by this energy.

I can try to ignore this fact. Seeking independence and individualism, I can deny that such a connection between me and others . . . between me and the universe . . . exists. Yet all my actions will continue to impact others. My teacher in school, whom I just described, was trying to live his life disconnected from me and his other students. Still, he had an impact on me. No man is an island.

Astrologers know that phases of the moon have an impact on our mood and our outlook, just as farmers know they play a role in planting and harvesting. People experience aches and pains when storms are brewing. Recurring thoughts of a particular person will plague me and then that person will call me on the phone seemingly out of the blue. Faithful prayers are answered. At the most basic level, when one of my loved ones hurts, I hurt with them. No one exists in a vacuum. We are all connected.

It is like the links in a chain. The chain is only as strong as the weakest link. I could turn that into this: I can only be as happy as the saddest person I know. Think of it this way. If there is someone in my sphere of existence who is chronically unhappy, cynical, depressed, or unfulfilled, no matter how hard I work at my own happiness and fulfillment, that person will drag me down. We have all experienced this. It could be a parent, spouse, child, friend, or coworker. Regardless of how much we try to focus on our own growth, the presence of this person, expressing their negative attitude, is a disruption. Sometimes we just choose to remove that person, if we can, from our sphere of existence. But often that extrication is not possible. And even if it is, chances are before too long we will run into a carbon copy. There are simply too many folks out there struggling on life's road, stuck in various stages of the journey and depressed or cynical about their inability to make progress or to satisfy the urges that will not go away. We can't run away from all of them.

It's like climbing a mountain together. We're all roped to one another. We will all get to a higher place if we just stop holding each other back. When we all climb together, we all benefit, because we're all connected . . . joined in this common pursuit. Teaching, then, is like leading someone up the mountain . . . helping them climb to the summit. When the student reaches the joyful height of a place where they've never been, the teacher is transported to that joyful place with them.

I have had many such experiences. Years ago, I taught swimming lessons. Children and adult nonswimmers alike would enter the shallow waters shaking like a leaf on a tree, unsure of themselves in this strange environment. But the children, who were far more playful, were soon splashing and frolicking and taking risks that enabled them to quickly learn how to leverage their body's natural buoyancy.

Adults were a different story. Grown men, twice my size and with children of their own who were my age, would cling to me like babies in three feet of water. White and stiffened with fear, almost to the point of rigor mortis, they sank like a rock unless I held them afloat.

The difference is the children were not yet under the dominion of the powerful dinosaur brain. At worst, they still had some balance between the left brain seeking security and the right brain seeking to play and explore. But the adults' heads were filled with the negative self-talk of the left brain. They had years of experience under their belts. They had seen or heard of all the drownings in the local lakes and rivers. Perhaps they had even experienced their own water-related trauma at some point in their lives. Their paradigms regarding the water were set in concrete. Water is dangerous. You will die in the water. It is not something to play around with.

So adults were much more difficult students than children. They were skeptical of my claim that they would float if they would simply relax. They didn't trust that I'd be by their side and would pull them to safety when necessary, if they'd only put their face in the water and attempt to float across the pool. Teaching adults to swim challenged me to think of every possible means at my disposal to help them get beyond their fears and discover the natural ability they were bottling up inside themselves. "You can swim. You just don't know it yet," I used to tell them.

And by the end of their lessons we all laughed and clapped with joy when they each one in turn swam unassisted across the **deep** end of the pool. They were elated by this achievement that only a couple weeks earlier, and perhaps for many years previously, they had firmly believed to be impossible. More importantly, I was just as elated. The satisfaction of knowing I had helped them exceed their expectations was a joyous experience for me.

In those moments, I felt an overwhelming sense of accomplishment . . . almost as if a voice from outside of me spoke the words, "Well done." It was the joy of fulfilling a portion of the life-purpose we all share. We are social, relational animals by design so that we can help each other. And when we do, we fulfill part of our purpose here.

It's like those peak experiences Maslow described in his theory of self-actualization in which we feel ecstasy, wonder, and awe. I was always awed by the process whereby those full-grown men were transformed from trembling babies into confident swimmers. I wondered at how I was able to be the catalyst for that transformation. And my joy at seeing them achieve it and knowing I played a part was nothing short of ecstasy. I felt important and needed, as though my existence really had purpose. They were lifted by their accomplishment. The experience increased their energy level. They were energized and as that heightened energy passed between us, I was energized right along with them. Because I was their helper . . . their teacher . . . I was lifted to a greater sense of well-being.

It was that result of the teaching experience, which I had as their teacher, that made it possible for me to start all over again with the next class. To hold the white-knuckled hands of the next beginner who was all bound up by the skepticism, fear, and distrust of me and the environment. To be patient with them as they struggled through the process, not of overcoming the water, but overcoming themselves . . . their own self-imposed boundaries, barriers, and limitations. To teach, coach, cajole, support, and comfort them, until finally the light would come on, the dinosaur brain would finally be retrained to believe "We can do this!" And they would be once and forevermore set free from those old bonds.

That's what happens for the truly engaged teacher. There's a bond formed between teacher and student that transcends all distinctions of race, creed, sex, economics, education, or career. When we put on our swimming suits and climbed into the pool, none of those outward symbols mattered. The water made us equals. The common energy that connected us one to another made us equals. We all fed off of that common energy, motivating and inspiring one another. And, as a result, all experienced rewards. That's what good teaching is all about.

This two-way reciprocal flow made them not only my students, but also my teachers. Each was different. Each had his or her own strengths and weaknesses. Through each new experience, resulting from all those differences, I discovered new resources inside me. As each in turn presented me with a different challenge to be overcome in order to enable his or her learning, I would dig deep and find that the answers really were there inside me. Even though I had never even thought about how to handle a particular situation before, the ideas seemed to be filed away in my unconscious mind just waiting to be called into action.

Mining our unconsciousness for the gems that hide there is by all accounts a difficult process. The entire psychiatric and psychological profession exists to carefully lead people through this precarious, sometimes painful, but always important endeavor toward unification and wholeness. Helping others learn and grow—teaching others—I have found to be one of the easiest ways to safely mine this part of our psyche. I get to know myself better when I attempt to enable others. When I try to understand their hesitations, it causes me to examine my own. When I look for ways to help them overcome problems, I find ways to overcome issues of my own. When I teach others, I discover strengths and abilities I never knew I had. I am at once both teacher and student. Teaching, without a doubt, can enable each one of us, regardless of our social status, job, or role in society, to further our own learning and growth . . . to have those peak, self-actualized experiences, and to continue our own journey closer and closer still to our one true self. This is what teaching does for you. This is why teachers need students. If you want to know yourself, and why you are here, then help others discover it for themselves.

Teachers I Have Known

Rainbows are people whose lives are bright, shining
examples for others. Shine on, shine on.
The world needs more people like you.

—Maya Angelou

Two

My personal journey has been filled with great teachers, some formal and several informal. A few stick out prominently in my memory as shining examples. These people made a difference in my life and, in so doing, taught me what it means to be a great teacher.

Mrs. Vera Isbill was my teacher twice in high school, first as a freshman, then again as a senior. In an era when nineteen was legal age, it seemed to be programmed that she would get her hands on you to wake you up when you started high school and again to polish you off before you headed out into the world. Mrs. Isbill's subject matter was English—composition in freshman year and literature in senior year—yet what she taught us went well beyond English. From the first moment Mrs. Isbill took hold of us, she began to peel back the film from our eyes to expose the possibilities in life.

This would have been a feat to accomplish with any group of thirteen- and fourteen-year-olds, but especially with us. Ours was a small country school nestled at the foot of the mountains in the quiet Tennessee hills. It was a humble existence. Most of us rode the school bus several miles from dirt farms where, with our families, we tended cows, pigs, and chickens to put meat on the dinner table; corn, hay, and alfalfa fields to feed the livestock; gardens and orchards for our own fruits and vegetables; horses for work and pleasure; and tobacco for our one cash crop.

Churches of all denominations could be found at the end of every country mile, as this was central to our lives in the heart of the Bible Belt. Our lives were filled with plenty. Still, we were devout farming people, segregated from the rest of the world by our economic conditions. Plato's *Allegory of the Cave* provides an accurate metaphor for our sheltered existence.

There were other forms of segregation found there too. In addition to being segregated from so much of the world by our remoteness and economics, we were segregated from one another by our religion. If you didn't attend the United Methodist Church, I wouldn't even know you existed until perhaps I ran across you in school. Even then we might not become friends, simply because you were not a member of my circle. I wouldn't see you and socialize with you outside of school the way I would my churchmates. The church and the families of two hundred or so members were my community. It began and ended within the boundaries of that safe cocoon. As a child, this literally created fear and distrust in my heart for anyone outside our circle.

I remember vividly an occasion when a lady came to sing at one of our revival services. Her sister was a member of our church. She, on the other hand, attended the Baptist church down the road. You could almost throw a rock and hit it from our Methodist parsonage. Yet it might as well have been on another planet. I was shocked that we were going to let her sing in our church. She was BAPTIST! How could we let her sing in the METHODIST church? Was that even legal? I wondered. I enjoyed her songs, although I silently prayed it wouldn't condemn my soul.

As bad as this form of segregation was, it was not the only form present. We were racially segregated as well. I wasn't even aware of it for the first twelve years of my life. I simply didn't know anyone who wasn't white, Anglo-Saxon, and protestant. Growing up in the early sixties, I literally never saw a person of color, not even in the few television shows we managed to pick up on the three local network channels beamed to the scrawny antenna perched high atop a tree beside our house in the hollow. When the word *nigger* was introduced into my vocabulary, I accepted it without question. It was just the normal thing to say. I was using the word long before I even knew what it meant.

This was our world. We were good, faithful, and hardworking people. At the same time we were poor, simple, narrow-minded, insulated, and isolated from reality. Maybe under different circumstances fourteen-year-old teenagers would be expected to have more open minds. With our situation, however, we came to high school not only steeled by the adult-size work on the farm, but also with very hardened paradigms—a condition usually found in adults with a few more years under their belts. This is how we were dumped at Mrs. Isbill's freshman English doorstep . . . confident and sure in our understanding of the world, but as blind as if we'd been raised in Plato's cave.

Mrs. Isbill was like the man, the teacher, who returned to the cave in Plato's allegory. He felt a responsibility, an obligation, to help the others reach the same enlightenment. So did Mrs. Isbill. She didn't have to devote her life to teaching. Her family was well-to-do. She married well. She didn't need that job at our little backwoods school. She did it, though. She didn't just teach freshman and senior English, either. *Au contraire!*

For one thing, Mrs. Isbill took it upon herself to devote her free time to exposing us to theater and performance art. She arranged the schoolwide talent show, and then insisted everyone with any semblance of talent must perform. She goaded onto the stage anyone who could walk and chew gum at the same time. So, when she learned that my classmate and I had sung together in church, there was no escaping. We won that talent show—two scared little freshman girls singing two-part harmony while banging out "Country Roads," "I Believe in Music," and "Torn Between Two Lovers" on the school's old out-of-tune piano—and already I was becoming inspired. My paradigms—my bonds— were already beginning to dissolve.

Mrs. Isbill arranged, produced, cast, and directed all the school plays, proving to us that anyone could act if they put their heart into it, let go, and had fun. This may all seem consistent with her role of English Literature teacher, but she didn't stop there. She also planned every year for the seniors to be exposed to several career days. Attorneys, politicians, businessmen, military leaders, college and university recruiters were all invited to visit the classroom. Bus trips were lined up to take us on tours of local colleges and university campuses. She prodded, pushed, and prepped us for the college entrance exam . . . us . . . who didn't even know there was such a thing.

That was just the tip of the iceberg. Mrs. Isbill devoted part of every single day to talk to us about our future. That's what she did. She simply talked to us. Believe it or not, I do remember studying English literature in her class. I still recall studying *Pygmalion* and *Great Expectations* and up until just a few years ago, when twenty-five years of trivia finally pushed it out of my memory, I could still recite some of the Old English introduction to the *Canterbury Tales* that she made us memorize.

My memory of all those works of literature has now dimmed. What hasn't dimmed, however, is the memory of Mrs. Isbill talking to us. I can still see her perched upon a stool in front of that classroom full of small wooden desks. Despite her pleasingly plump, barely over five-feet frame, she presided over us like a queen on her throne. In fact, she pointed out the distinctly Roman arch in her nose and the curve of her fingernails, which always made us giggle.

Mrs. Isbill talked to us about life, told us her entire life story, multiple times over (including the hard lessons she had learned). She told us about former students, country kids just like us, who had risen to great heights, told us about things happening in the world that we had never considered possible, asked us what we wanted to do with our lives, challenged us when we didn't know, or didn't care, or if we were selling ourselves short. She assured us that we were all, each and every one of us, capable of great things that we had yet to imagine.

Mrs. Isbill inspired us. In so doing, she challenged and destroyed our paradigms. She led us out of the cave. For generations of students, Mrs. Isbill was much more than just a teacher of English composition and literature. Because of her inspiration, we are now the doctors, lawyers, politicians, successful businessmen and businesswomen, military leaders, good citizens, spouses and parents, and yes, enlightened, engaged, inspiring teachers. With every fiber of her being, Mrs. Isbill was an inspiration and for as long as my memory remains intact, she always will be.

Wayne Erwin was my first basketball coach. What a challenge that must have been for him. Our little school out in the country drew kids who spent more time in the tobacco patch than on the basketball court, although there was little difference since one was found in the dirt right beside the other.

When Coach Erwin arrived he found that our feeble dribbling, unorthodox shooting, and lazy play had resulted in several years of losing seasons. We flopped around lackadaisically in the small gymnasium, which doubled as a cafeteria—our *cafenasium* we fondly called it—totally oblivious to our reputation.

But Coach Erwin knew. He had already endured the jeering and jokes from fellow coaches upon receiving the appointment. Little did we know that Coach Erwin was on a mission. Our world and our perspective of it were about to change.

Coach Erwin had grown up in an area where basketball was a proud tradition. When he walked into the room, the atmosphere changed. He exuded the pride he wanted to instill in us. I remember vividly the day he stood in the middle of the gym with all of us gathered around.

"The other coaches laughed at me for coming here. They made fun of our gym . . . joked about our record . . . jeered about our lack of talent. Well, that all stops today! No one will ever make fun of us again!"

I literally felt the pride and determination well up inside me. Coach Erwin instantly became our role model.

We began with the gym. It wasn't long before Coach had organized our parents into a booster club. They had barbecue dinners to raise money for paint, and for a few months parents and kids alike became painters. We decided our school colors, which had always been red and white, needed some pizzazz, so we added blue. I shall never forget the day my teammates and I spilled a gallon of that blue paint in the middle of the hard tile cafenasium floor. That day we did more cleaning than painting. Through it all, though, we had fun.

In parallel, Coach Erwin was teaching us the fundamentals of basketball, but we were learning something far more important. We were learning to take pride in what we did. For the first time we had pride in our school, our game, our skills, our team play, our tiny little red, white, and blue gym, and most of all in ourselves. We exhibited that pride in everything we did. We practiced late into the evening, but still studied and made straight As in school. On the weekends we walked or had our parents drive us to the nearest neighbors to sell candy, shampoo, wrapping paper, trinkets, whatever fund-raising material we could find. With the money we raised, for the first time ever, both the boy's and the girl's team had warm-ups to wear over our uniforms. These were not just any warm-ups. They were special, for the material was purchased with the money we had raised. Moreover, they were handmade by one of our parents, a seamstress, who carefully measured each one of us and tailored the beautiful red, white, and blue warm-ups to our unique specifications.

When we stepped onto the court for our first game that season, no one laughed. Our gym was sparkling. Our uniforms were perfect. Our warm-up drills were crisp, and our play was intense. We had evolved in a few short months from chubby, lazy little farm kids into proud student-athletes. Coach Erwin had instilled that pride in all of us, from the youngest to the oldest, from the worst to the best player, and from the first to the last parent.

More importantly, Coach Erwin taught us the importance of hard work. If you're going to do something, give it all you've got, seemed to be the underlying theme. Nothing is free. Nothing comes without effort . . . not the clean new gym, or the new uniforms, or the winning record, or even a spot on the starting team . . . you have to work for it.

It was not that we had not already learned about pride and hard work. Life on the farm was filled with hard work. I thought I was being tortured when Daddy dragged us to the tobacco patch in the wee hours of the morning and kept us there until dark. Once we were there, we were certainly expected to take pride in our work and do the job right. Lollygagging, as my daddy referred to goofing off, was simply not tolerated. Still, the important lesson was not fully learned in those fields. The farm was Daddy's enterprise. It wasn't mine. I didn't feel any ownership. I was just being obedient to his dominion over me. Had it not been for my experience on the basketball team with Coach Erwin, I don't know if I would have learned that important lesson.

Coach Erwin made sure we learned the lesson of working with all your physical and mental attributes to be all that you can be. When school adjourned for the summer, he gave us workout schedules to follow each and every day: run one mile; jump rope five hundred times; perform thirty minutes of exercises, thirty minutes of ball handling drills, thirty minutes of passing drills, and one hour of shooting practice.

After that first summer of diligent practice, I blossomed into a basketball player. I may have only been twelve years old, but my college basketball scholarship was earned in that one summer. Fans who had watched me fumble around the court the previous year were amazed at the transformation. What they didn't know was how deep that change went. Not only had the physical skills they could see on the surface been transformed, my entire psyche was transformed.

Coach Erwin gave us more than just a workout schedule to follow. He gave us inspirational materials to read and study, with this one assignment . . . when we returned to school in the fall, we were required to have memorized one of the motivational poems. It was to become our mantra. One in particular, which now floats around on the Internet variously attributed to different authors, became my own and sticks with me even to this day, decades later:

The Man Who Thinks He Can!

If you think you're beaten, you are;
If you think you dare not, you don't!
If you'd like to win, but think you can't,
It's almost a cinch that you won't.

If you think you'll lose, you're lost
For out in the world we find
Success begins with a fellow's will;
It's all in the state of mind!

If you think you're outclassed, you are;
You've got to think high to rise.

You've got to be sure of yourself
before you can win the prize.

Life's battles don't always go
To the strongest or fastest man;
But sooner or later the man who wins
Is the man who thinks he can!

From Coach Erwin we learned that success in life, as in basketball, required dedication and hard work to continually improve. We also learned that it need not be any other way, because the sense of pride that results from the hard-earned success and recognition of your efforts is immeasurable. That realization has proven to be the single most important factor in all my subsequent decisions and accomplishments.

Coach Erwin challenged us. He challenged us to rise above the limitations of our facility, our funding, our past history, and even our own individual abilities. He challenged us to do more, be more, and achieve more. Then he coached us in how to do that one step at a time. The resulting appreciation for hard work and pride in our diligent effort has stuck with me ever since. I have Coach Erwin to thank for that.

Mrs. Josephine Black was my piano teacher extraordinaire. I guess my parents must have mistaken my constant pounding on the keys of my grandparents' old upright piano as raw talent. So, beginning in the second grade, I had the pleasure of taking private piano lessons from Mrs. Black. Once a week, she would drive several miles from her house in the city to our small school out in the country. She was like a ray of sunshine penetrating the thick forest of our country existence.

Mrs. Black was a character. Her slightly squat and plump body, teetering on spike heels, was topped off by a silvery white Marilyn Monroe wig. Bleached a little whiter and teased a bit higher than Marilyn would have worn it, the silver hair swooped down in dramatic fashion across one side of Mrs. Black's mid-fifties face.

Like Mrs. Black's demeanor, the wig was never exactly secure or straight, and instead seemed to move from one position to the next throughout the day. Sometimes she even appeared to tilt her head back slightly in order to see from underneath the mass of migrating hair. With her plump hands, adorned by sparkling dinner rings and long pink fingernails that clicked on the piano keys when she played, she would hold her hair with one hand while pecking out a tune for me with the other.

Summertime was even more interesting, because then my mom drove me to Mrs. Black's little white house for my lessons. I felt like Alice in Wonderland stepping through the looking glass. When I walked underneath the green-and-white striped awning into Mrs. Black's living room, I was captivated. This city home was not anything like our farmhouse. The fancy living room furniture with curved wooden legs, the gleaming wooden tables, the sparkling lamps, exquisite china, and rich, black piano were beautiful to me. Even the smell in the house was different, transporting me into another world while I was in Mrs. Black's house.

Unfortunately, I was a terrible piano player. My musical ability started and stopped with a good ear and singing voice. I had been belting out songs at church right alongside people three and four times my age for years. But my short, stubby fingers were just never meant to play the piano. Despite the fact that I quickly learned to read music and could sing the songs with ease, the connection between my brain and my fingers seemed severed when I attempted to play. I knew I wasn't going to be a pianist when I heard my friends at school playing fluidly and flawlessly in their lessons.

Still, I never heard those words from Mrs. Black. You'd never have known from her that any of us were not virtuosos. All we ever received from Mrs. Black was unconditional love and acceptance. Her signature hot-pink lipstick applied liberally to her plump lips and, like her wig, never quite straight—a little almost always smeared across her front teeth—framed a broad, approving smile that never left her pleasant face.

Mrs. Black never had children of her own. We were her children. As she hugged me close, her softness enfolding me, I felt so special. She made me feel like her best student. When annual recital time rolled around, she beamed with pride as she sent each one of us onstage to bang out our best rendition of "Mary Had a Little Lamb," "Turkey in the Straw," "I'd Like to Teach the World to Sing," and "My Country Tis of Thee." No matter how many sour notes we hit, she showered us with affection and praise when we came offstage.

I thought I would never want to stop taking lessons for this very reason. However, as time went on and I grew older, practice became more of a chore and my ability was definitely not improving. The time had come to give up on the piano dream. Nevertheless, Mrs. Black gave me something much more important than piano skills. I did learn from her, a lot more than I ever expected.

Years later, after excelling in math skills throughout school and into my career, I heard about research that had been conducted with young students. One group was given piano lessons, while the control group was not. During the research, the math and logic skills of the two groups were studied. The group of students receiving piano lessons showed dramatically better performance in math skills than the control group who didn't receive the lessons. Studies such as these had shown a link between the brain conditioning that occurs when learning to play the piano and the all-important math and logic skills.

I smiled at this revelation. Who would've thought that such an unlikely eccentric as Mrs. Black had unwittingly made such an impact on my life and even been instrumental in setting me on a path to a successful business career? As I listened to the report describing the results of the study, I knew one thing for certain. Had it not been for Mrs. Black's attitude and approach, I wouldn't have had the chance to learn those important lessons. If she hadn't loved and accepted me, despite the fact that I couldn't play a lick, and continually encouraged me, I never would have stayed in her program. The lessons—both obvious and hidden—would have rolled off me like water off a duck's back.

Gordon Inscore was a special man. Several generations who grew up in my neck of the woods knew him affectionately as Go-Go. It was the best pronunciation of Gordon that a small child had been able to muster years earlier, and it had simply stuck. Go-Go and his cousin Roy had married sisters, Theresa and Faye, and had taken up running the small country store, Colyer and Inscore's General Merchandise.

The store was the hub of our small country community. Built entirely of wood worn smooth from years of business traffic and loafing, the old building was straight out of the Old West with traditional stairstep-shaped marquee storefront, flat roof, and full-length wood-slatted porch down the front. The only modernization was the red and white paint, enough electrical wiring to support the old wooden coolers, and a few bare light bulbs hung from the ceiling. A solitary gas pump stood at one end of the long porch like a one-armed sentry.

The store sat right on the road with barely enough space for cars to pull over underneath the high front porch, which was perched about four or five feet in the air. Built back into a small hill on one corner of a four-way intersection, two large four-foot square windows framed the screen door at the front, and one more small side window near the back of the store sat just above ground level of the hill outside.

Warmed on cool days by the small potbelly coal stove tucked in the front corner, the store was a gathering place. Long, wooden benches, their seats worn as smooth as glass, lined the three walls around the stove, and it was rare to walk in and not find old farmers swapping tall tales and community news. The smell of coal smoke, leather work boots, hardware, breads and cakes, grain and animal feed, and aging wooden boards joined to produce a heady bouquet not to be found anywhere else. Combined with these unique aromas, the dimly lit atmosphere was almost mysterious, with strange treasures tucked away in every nook and cranny. But there was nothing dim or mysterious about one thing—the bright ear-to-ear smile on Go-Go's face and the twinkle in his eye that greeted anyone who walked through the door.

Standing about six feet tall, Go-Go seemed ageless. He was always the same. Unathletic and jiggly, Go-Go's chubby frame fit snuggly into the khaki or olive twill work pants he wore. His long leather belt wrapped high around the widest expanse of his waistline at the point where his plaid cotton shirts were neatly tucked. Go-Go's thinning salt and pepper hair was carefully combed over his balding head, capping off a welcoming face. Seeing his thick, full lips in an ever-present smile was so natural that it never seemed to leave his face, and his warm eyes sparkled from underneath his thick eyebrows.

Go-Go moved around the store with steps as tender as a cautious grandmother moving about her kitchen. At the slightest provocation, he would as easily as a child burst into an almost silent laughter that caused his entire body to bounce up and down until tears of joy rolled down his ruddy cheeks. Go-Go was one of those characters who constantly made you wonder what funny observation he would make next. He saw the humor and joy in every minute of every day.

From his regular perch behind the long, smooth counter—bookended by the over-sized wooden cash register on one end and the large roll of white waxed paper on the other end that was used to wrap fresh-cut cheeses and meats—Go-Go was much more than just our grocer. Go-Go was the heart of our community. He ran tabs for families down on their luck, delivered groceries to the doors of the elderly and shut-in residents of the community, laughed with the happy, cried with the sad, and counseled the downtrodden. Whether from behind the store counter or behind the pulpit as Sunday School Superintendent at our nearby church, Go-Go made all the members of our small community feel like we were part of something special—something bigger than ourselves and our simple country lives.

Go-Go especially loved children. With no children of his own, he adopted every child in the community. Once you walked into the store, you were a member of his family. There's no telling how many free suckers, ice cream, and Cokes Go-Go gave away over the years, which would later be replaced by a Bible with your name engraved on the front and a handwritten letter of encouragement if you were one of the fortunate few who made it off to college.

No question about it. Go-Go loved and nurtured us all. Yet it wasn't until I had reached middle age, and Go-Go was an old man, that I realized the full extent to which his love and acceptance reached. For many years, I'd never seen Go-Go in any context other than running the store, supervising our Sunday School, or watching basketball games at our small school. I had forgotten that he'd also served for many years as a bailiff in the local criminal court. Then one day my turn came to serve as a juror.

Nervous about the prospect, I was greeted by that familiar, broad smile when I walked into the courtroom. Go-Go's chubby body looked strange to me in the khaki-and-olive drab bailiff's uniform, his badge shining on his chest. It felt like an episode of Andy Griffith, where Otis might have squeezed into Barney's uniform.

I was tickled to death to see Go-Go, and ran to his side to receive the familiar hug and instruction that only he could give. It was as if he'd been placed there just for me, to ease my anxiety. Soon, however, I knew that it wasn't Go-Go but I who had been placed there for a reason . . . so I could learn an important lesson.

> One of the signs of maturity is the birth of a sense of fellowship with other human beings as we take our place amont them.
> – Virginia Woolf

I sat quietly in the back of the courtroom watching as Go-Go treated everyone with the same caring and respect I had come to expect from him. Black or white, red or yellow, male or female, rich or poor, clean or dirty, educated or illiterate . . . it didn't matter who walked through the door into that courtroom. His lips spread into that genuine smile, and each felt special in his presence. I realized through that experience that Go-Go's love and acceptance of others didn't stop with me. It didn't even stop with the members of our small community. Go-Go showered it, indiscriminately, upon everyone with whom he came in contact.

I learned more than the criminal justice process in that courtroom. I learned that Go-Go was more than just the heart of our community. I learned what showing unconditional love and acceptance of others truly means. From the potbellied stove at the store, to the church, to the courtroom, I saw firsthand how it broke through the barriers of fear, distrust, uncertainty, worry, and defensiveness to create an opening to receive Go-Go's valuable wisdom and guidance.

This passage may surprise you. The teacher I'm praising here is not a person at all but rather that great teacher, experience. I went to work in a manufacturing facility when I was nineteen years old. What was intended to be a summer job during a break from college, however, turned into a twenty-one-year career. Over that span of time, while balancing continuation of formal education, work, and everyday life, I learned a great deal about the importance of structure and organization.

Still, if I thought the degree of organization required to navigate my personal life was high, it paled in comparison to the structure and organization in place at the manufacturing facility. Walking into the factory was like stepping onto another planet. Initially, I was merely lost and intimidated, but quickly fell into the rhythms that enabled work to flow smoothly in the operation.

Those predictable rhythms were enabled by a clear organizational structure. While hierarchical, and some might argue staid and stale, it provided much-needed order to our lives on this planet. The defined roles and responsibilities helped clarify who needed to do what in order to get the job done right. Roles and responsibilities were linked to the organizational mission, which was in turn linked to a corporate strategy. This structure explained where we were trying to go and what role we each played to get us there. How we worked together to get there was described in policies, procedures, and work instructions. These written guidelines organized our work. Redundant effort was eliminated.

Activities were coordinated. Everyone had suppliers and customers, with each person's output serving as input to the next person in the end-to-end process. The factory hummed with a symphony of activity, and work flowed through the facility like a mighty river.

To those who've never worked in such an environment, the whole concept of structures and processes may sound extremely constricting and restraining. Nothing could be farther from the truth. The structure and organization is facilitative. It's what enables the effort and creativity of each individual to add value every step of the way. This point was never more clear in my mind than when the moving story of Apollo 13 was revived and shared with a global audience on the big screen.

In 1995, Imagine Entertainment released the Brian Grazer produced film *Apollo 13*, directed by Ron Howard. This movie introduced a new generation to the miraculous 1970 flight of NASA's thirteenth Apollo mission.

After having just beaten the Russians in the race to the moon with Neal Armstrong's famous moonwalk, sentiment in this country toward the next Apollo flight was lackluster and ambivalent. Making the situation more tense, the crew slated to make the mission was grounded when Commander Alan Shepard developed an ear infection. This began what appeared to be a string of bad luck as Jim Lovell's crew was bumped up, leaving them a mere six months to prepare for the demanding mission.

Then Lovell, who was making his last flight as a commander, unexpectedly watched helplessly along with crew member Fred Haise as their third crewman and pilot, Ken Mattingly, tested positive for measles and was grounded only two days before launch. Scrambling to salvage the mission by bringing in backup pilot, Jack Swigert, flight director Gene Krantz could not see the omen presented by the fact that the Apollo 13 flight would launch at 1300 hours and 13 minutes, entering the moon's gravity on April 13.

Disaster struck almost immediately when, during the launch, the number five center engine shut down. Completing liftoff and escape from earth's gravity by burning the remaining four engines longer than normal, the flight crew and staff at Mission Control in Houston thought the problems were over. They had only just begun.

Once in space and enroute to their designated landing zone on the moon's surface, the crew, inside the Odyssey Command Module, stepped through well-practiced procedures to continually monitor and manage the spacecraft's maneuverability and performance. It was during one of these routine procedures, on day three, April 13, two hundred miles above the earth, that a damaged coil in an oxygen tank sparked an explosion, blowing out the tank along with an entire panel on the service module and venting the precious remaining oxygen gas into space. When the explosion rocked the craft, warning lights, alarms, and sirens flashed, glared, and blasted away inside the Command Module, as the entire ship lurched and rolled out of control and farther off course, thus eliciting the now famous phrase from commander Lovell, "Houston, we have a problem."

Two fuel cells were gone and the spaceship was quickly losing power. Even after they regained control of the ship, it was clear they would not walk on the moon. What little power remained had to be conserved, for in an instant the objective of the mission had changed. The new objective was to avert the unthinkable and to return to earth alive.

A world that had only three days earlier been uninterested in the space flight was now united by the drama. Television broadcasts were dominated by the status updates and commentary. Schools held rallies. Churches sponsored prayer vigils. The Pope led a special Mass. The common man joined in unison to will the men back home to their loved ones.

Nowhere was that unison more strong than at NASA Mission Control. After an initial period of shock and chaos, flight director Kranz mobilized his team. Focusing them on working systematically through the problem rather than guessing, he guided them safely back to their clearly defined and understood roles, responsibilities, and procedures. Any misperceptions about the effect of such structure and organization, such as suggesting it creates a restrictive environment, is erased when watching the unfolding reenactment of this drama. NASA's structure and organization provided a framework within which the ingenuity of the brilliant scientists could be put to its most effective use in the most expeditious manner, thereby preserving each precious second that would be needed to save the astronauts' lives.

Power was completely shut down in the Odyssey Command Module to conserve energy, and the crewmen moved to the Aquarius Lunar Module to use it as a lifeboat. In the Lunar Module, which was designed only for short flights in outer space, with skin only as thick in some places as a couple layers of tinfoil, the crew soon became severely cold and sleep deprived. While the ship drifted powerlessly through space, drawn merely by the earth's gravitational pull, down on earth each member of Mission Control, including grounded crewman Ken Mattingly, worked feverishly to improvise a new mission to return the crippled craft.

Scientists moved rapidly, adapting procedures to fit unpredictable situations as they arose. A carbon dioxide filter was improvised when toxic gas in the Lunar Module reached dangerously high levels. The trajectory of the craft's tumble was corrected using an impro-vised manual procedure with only the visual orientation of the earth through a tiny trian-gular window in the Lunar Module as a guide. This gave the ship its only hope of hitting the miniscule two-and-a-half degree reentry corridor and preventing it from simply bouncing off the earth's atmosphere with no power left to get home.

When the cold, sick, and scared crew, holding the new reentry and landing proce-dures from Mission Control, eventually powered up the Command Module and jettisoned the Service and Lunar Modules, the world sat glued to the unfolding story. The heat shield had been damaged by the blast, to what degree was unknown. The module could quite possibly never withstand the heat of reentering the earth's atmosphere. It was also not known if the parachutes were still functional. Even if the module survived the heat of reentry, it might crash into the South Pacific at a deadly three hundred miles per hour. If this wasn't enough to worry about, a typhoon warning threatened the landing zone off the coast of Iwo Jima.

Apollo 13, the mission that launched on April 11, 1970, would return to earth on the morning of April 17, if their luck would only take a turn for the better. All television viewers and members of Mission Control collectively held their breath when the typical three-minute radio blackout during reentry stretched beyond four minutes. Then all exhaled in one great sigh of relief when the module burst into view with all three para-chutes floating on the gentle South Pacific breeze. As Mission Control broke into cheers and tears, it was clear that Lady Luck had finally smiled upon the Apollo 13 mission. More importantly, so had the genius and determination of every member of the NASA team.

Supported by the structure and procedures on which the organization was built, each person was enabled to contribute what they knew best to the success of the revised mission. Just as I experienced in the factory, within that structure, they had the framework to become flexible . . . to improvise . . . while avoiding chaos. What could have been NASA's biggest disaster up to that point in history was turned into its finest hour. This is truly a lesson in the importance of structure and organization.

When I first met Lynn Whipple, we were both employed as directors—he in Human Resources and I in Service—in a large, international corporation. "Call me Lynn or Whip, but please don't call me Mr. Whipple." Lynn smiled, referring to the wimpy main character in the old Charmin television commercials.

We had asked Lynn to join our team because of his recent experience restructuring the engineering group located in our region. Having just formed a team comprised of our organization's senior managers, we recognized that the service landscape in which we operated was changing dramatically, requiring a new strategy that would challenge the very structure of our organization as well.

Restructuring an organization always impacts people. After all, it is the people who perform the work of the organization. It was only logical for us to get input from a human resource professional like Lynn who was experienced in the inevitable work of redefining jobs, conducting selection and placement of new and existing employees, and managing the transition of employees whose jobs were eliminated by the restructuring. That was what I expected to get from Lynn. I can now reflect on the fact that what I received from him was so much more than expected . . .

The time for the clock to change from standard to daylight saving time was fast approaching. On this early October evening, I noticed the sun seemed to hang lower and lower in the sky with each passing day. Like a bright orange spotlight, it beamed at westbound motorists as they tried to shield their eyes. What a nuisance it was this time of year! We had grown accustomed to it and had come to expect those piercing sunbeams. Still, we groaned and complained as we struggled to fight through it.

Today was no different, as I pulled from my street into the thoroughfare. When the sun hit my eyes, I went into defensive mode, slapping the sun visor down and grabbing my sunglasses from the console in one well-practiced motion. It occurred to me then that it wouldn't be so bad. The tiny hamlet where I was driving sat in a lake basin surrounded by the Smoky Mountain foothills. Large oak and maple trees shaded the roadway from the yards of the historic homes, churches, and family businesses along the way, allowing only an occasional splattering of sunlight to seep through.

As I drove along, I thought of Lynn. He had been gone for about a week. I was sure he had completed his drive now from Tennessee to Utah where he was embarking on a new career. His departure was still fresh, and I hadn't yet overcome the strange feeling of walking by his empty office knowing he wasn't there . . . wouldn't be back. I imagined Lynn at the moment, despite the time difference, standing in the evening sun. He would not have the benefit of close foothills or looming woodlands to block the sun's rays. The setting sun would be cutting across the salt flats of Utah like a laser, full-on and relentless, not like the brief flashes that were peeping through the treetops as I drove along.

I didn't imagine Lynn, however, rushing into a defensive posture against the sun's rays. No visors, sunglasses, or umbrellas to shield him. He wouldn't view it as a nuisance. Instead, I imagined Lynn looking confidently straight into the light, a smile spreading across his round face, his sandy-red hair shining against the sun's rays, his ice-blue eyes soaking up the light as though he could capture it and carry it around with him only to release it at some future time through his penetrating gaze. That was the way I would remember Lynn . . . never closed or defensive to the light, but always open to it, seeking it, craving the light . . . the truth . . . that so many others go to such great lengths to avoid.

It took some time for me to learn this from Lynn. I didn't always work directly with him, but I was aware of him. It was kind of like the mountains nearby that surrounded us. I'm aware of them, but I don't always take note and appreciate them. That's how it was between Lynn and me for several years. Occasionally I did notice his calmness that seemed to stem from a deep knowing and assurance that he was on the right path. At least, that was how it seemed with Lynn, and I envied that.

I had been creeping toward my midlife crisis and had been overwhelmed by the feeling that there was something else, something more, that I was supposed to be doing. Yet what exactly that might be escaped me. I was only beginning to realize that the life vision I was born to fulfill was tugging at my heart.

Unfortunately, this growing awareness did nothing for the anxiety I was starting to feel regarding my daily occupation. In fact, it redoubled it. The feeling of unfulfilled purpose rose, as I disdained more and more my lack of effective initiative to discover it. The people around me, I observed, seemed perfectly content having found their calling . . . especially Lynn. He carried himself with an air of calmness and confidence that I greatly admired.

Ironically, this also made being around Lynn very uncomfortable. He had this irritating way of always being right, which frustrated me to no end. Maybe it was not frustration at all, but perhaps it was envy. He had what I wanted. I wasn't quite sure what it was yet. I just knew he had it, and I didn't. That made me so intimidated by him, as if his *knowing* were something he had captured by his own personal might.

I now understand, it was that wonder, awe, and envy of Lynn's unwavering commitment to his life vision that dissolved all my arrogance, pretenses, and paradigms, making me totally open like a sponge to whatever it was that I could learn from him.

I learned many things from Lynn. He taught us about change. He made us aware that people go through intense feelings of betrayal and denial when subjected to change. Externalizing and venting is normal, even healthy, during these periods and should be understood and supported.

> The final test of a leader is that he leaves behind him in others the conviction and the will to carry on.
> – Walter Lippmann

Lynn made us realize that we were a dysfunctional team, and he taught us how to communicate more effectively with one another—that if we treated each other with high levels of respect, empathy, genuineness, and specificity we could avoid uncomfortable and unnecessary conflict. He taught us how to celebrate our diversity, by seeking first to understand before trying to be understood. Lynn showed us not only in word but also in deed how to be an effective team of diverse individuals through agreement on mission, goals, roles, responsibilities, and our processes for working together.

Most importantly, Lynn taught us that it's possible to find meaning and purpose through our work—meaning that goes beyond simple financial gain. He convinced us that it wasn't only possible but that it was okay. We were not abandoning any of our business obligations by doing so, nor were we jeopardizing the company's success in any way. Quite to the contrary, if more than just our hands—if also our hearts—were engaged, we were actually increasing the likelihood that together we would reach our fullest potential and achieve our corporate objective to generate positive financial results for the company.

Still, that's not the reason for doing it, according to Lynn. The reason for doing it, he explained, is because it's right. Lynn espoused the motto of "doing right things" as more important than doing things right.

He constantly reminded us, "It doesn't have to be this way. We can change it. We can make it better for each other."

He knew, and he made us believe that our work is not that thing we do to make money, which prevents us from doing what we love. Work is that thing we do which enables us to do what we love.

Lynn believes we each are born with a vision that we can achieve in this lifetime.

Too often we view our work as a hindrance to achieving that vision. However, when we allow ourselves to begin to view our work instead as an enabler, wonderful, unexpected things can happen to us.

Lynn exemplified that our lives can be enriched even at work. We don't have to be two different people—the person at work and the other person at home. We can have both. Lynn understood that. He helped us understand it too.

Yes, Lynn not only taught us about these things, he demonstrated them every day. I developed a great admiration for his ability to practice, seemingly without fail, the concepts he preached. Despite being a good teacher, Lynn once related to me why he preferred a permanent role in a large corporation, rather than a consulting position.

"I don't want to just waltz in, talk about all this nice stuff then waltz out," Lynn explained. "I want to be a part of the change. I want to be involved."

Lynn was more than just our teacher. Lynn was our leader.

I finally realized that just as we defend ourselves from the sun's piercing rays, we also hide from the bright light of truth in this life. But people like Lynn are drawn to it like a moth to the flame. It is Lynn's greatest strength . . . and as I would also soon learn . . . it is his enormous burden.

I knew that all our team members appreciated Lynn's talents. We marveled over his gift of leadership and teaching, and his determination to continually promote those high ideals. I expected that everyone in the company felt the same about him as we did. At first, everyone I talked with did. Then gradually I began to see signs of something else.

I knew some people were taken aback by Lynn's assuredness and conviction . . . intimidated by him as I had initially been. Yet somehow it had failed to help them see what he had to offer. Others just misunderstood him, I presumed. So gradually I gained a new awareness. There were apparently pockets of people in the organization who didn't appreciate Lynn the way we did. They didn't hang on his every word like we did. They didn't "ooh" and "aah" over every tidbit of wisdom he imparted. In fact, for every one person I found who subscribed to Lynn's teachings and philosophies, there was at least one if not more who were either dead set against it or simply oblivious to a better way of working.

It was as if two entirely different cultures existed in the company. I was glad to belong to the group that listened to and learned from people like Lynn. I knew that a lack of full acceptance from everyone didn't make Lynn wrong. I also began to realize we were in the minority. What's worse, I discovered that this often created very uncomfortable circumstances for Lynn.

I was astonished to learn that while he could stand in front of us with such consistency and teach the powerful concepts that were transforming our organization, all the while he was being pressured to back off and conform to the way it had been before he started rocking the boat. Thankfully, Lynn didn't conform and remained true to his life vision. We'd gone too far and seen too much to give up and go back to the way things had been. We were like starving orphans being allowed to feast at a well-laid table for the first time. For the moment, we had no thought for whose burden it had been to spread that feast before us, or even that it had been a labor at all. It was Lynn who shouldered that burden for us, even after it was clear that he might ostracize himself by doing so.

Lynn seemed more superhuman to me than ever before. What was it about him that made him realize that the concepts he taught were worth fighting for—were even worth risking his job for? I became increasingly curious to know more about Lynn, the man. What was it at the very core of his being that made him unwavering in his dedication to bringing about this certain kind of growth in all the people he met?

It wasn't difficult to find out. Lynn welcomed the opportunity. Like a child with a wonderful secret, he wanted people to ask . . . to give him the opportunity to share it. Lynn smiled across the lunch table at me as he began to answer my questions.

"I'm a seventh generation member of the Church of Latter Day Saints," Lynn told me. "It's not that the church is a big part of my life . . . the church *is* my life." Lynn looked at me intently with those penetrating eyes.

A slight shiver went up my spine when I realized the serious nature of the discussion my questions had spawned. I listened intently as Lynn continued for several minutes to explain the foundation of his religion, the depth of faith, and how it underscored all his interactions with other human beings, until finally the waitress took away his cold meal. He had been so engrossed he hadn't eaten a bite.

I looked at Lynn in amazement. When someone has the conviction and courage to stand up for what they believe in, that must be respected even if you don't share their beliefs.

"How can you do it?" I wondered aloud. "How can you have a faith and a commitment to your life purpose and religious foundation this strong and still come to work *here* every day? Why aren't you out teaching and ministering to others? How can you resist telling everyone you come into contact with about it, when your faith is so central in your life?"

The two—conviction to a life vision such as his and working in a large corporation—seemed diametrically opposed to me.

Lynn seemed caught off guard for a moment. Then he smiled and began to explain. It was a very complex and personal explanation, yet Lynn freely gave it. He looked me square in the eye as he talked.

"If you want to know the answers that God has for you, just ask him. Ask him, and he will tell you, just as he made the vision for my life known to me."

Lynn recounted his life experiences that explained how he knew with all his heart that he was fulfilling God's vision for him . . . to help others see that there is a better way . . . that we can see the best in one another . . . and we can make the world a better place for each other. Lynn had never preached his religion in the workplace. He had never acted holier-than-thou or even mentioned his personal creed. Yet he had made a monumental difference in all of us who learned from him, simply because he had lived his beliefs every day without fail.

Suddenly, the puzzle pieces fell into place. I had listened to Lynn talk about work being one of the vehicles to enable the fulfillment of your life vision. That idea had never been more real to me than it was at that moment. No wonder Lynn was so unwavering in his commitment to the ideals that were obviously guiding his choices at work. No wonder he was so consistently true to the same message, regardless of any criticism, discouragement, or lack of appreciation he encountered. No wonder he had such a positive impact on us.

Lynn's message went well beyond mere job descriptions or company policies and procedures. Lynn saw beyond all that. What Lynn saw was other human beings desiring to engage their hearts and hands in something meaningful and his life vision for helping them do it. Through Lynn, I learned to see it too.

Dr. Bill Cox, a retired military officer, teacher of research in my Master's program, and chairman of that department at the local college, could easily have fallen victim to an egocentric posture. After all, he possesses a knowledge and experience to which few can lay claim. But Dr. Cox is not egocentric at all. Instead, he is a teacher who makes the all-important connection with his students.

To begin with, although the weighty nature of his subject matter could easily result in mild to major arrogance, Dr. Cox doesn't take himself too seriously. Research is no easy topic nor is it generally regarded as a fun topic. It involves the use of statistics and application of a structure so cumbersome and so left-brained that it virtually prevents any right-brain creativity from ever emerging. Just do the research, draw conclusions, and state the findings. With these strikes against them right out of the gate, research instructors can be oft-maligned individuals. Not Dr. Cox. He is beloved by his current and former students.

Despite the dry subject matter, Dr. Cox makes it fun. Looking like a mischievous little boy, defying the slight wrinkles in his face and graying blond hair, in front of his class his blue eyes twinkle when the grin flashes on his face.

As we joked our way through the subject matter, Dr. Cox understood what a stress relieving activity humor was for us, because he had quickly connected with us. He knew us as individuals . . . as equals. That was no small feat.

Our group was made up of a Native American artist, an insurance claims representative, a Baptist minister, an Air National Guard Major, a real estate title agent, a technical school guidance counselor, a director of a corporation, a professional fund-raiser, a college admissions counselor, and a high school swimming coach. Our personalities, perspectives, and previous experience with the subject matter were as diverse as the colors on a color wheel. Dr. Cox intuitively recognized this and made us comfortable, nonetheless, from day one.

He quickly gauged our level of comfort, or lack thereof, with the content. Then he structured the class so that we were either helping one another in a small group format, or he was circulating the room giving us individual instruction. His office door was always open as were the phone lines to his home, office, and cell phone. Dr. Cox made himself approachable and accessible to each of us—in person, over the phone, and via e-mail—for specialized, individual assistance, and this was quite a commitment given that the course and application of the concepts to our own research projects stretched over several months. No question was too trivial. No issue too great. Dr. Cox never belittled the student . . . never failed to help. He connected with us in a way that made it possible for him to have empathy for our confusion and our own unique personal trials.

Empathy has been referred to as the ability to be fully with someone even in his or her darkest moment. That is exactly what Dr. Cox did for me. Personal crisis struck early in the Master's program and plagued me throughout the completion of my research project. As every facet of my life was turned upside down, I often wondered if I would have the fortitude to hold together and finish the program. Conducting stellar research and producing grade A work that would be used to help develop the new student research guide was the farthest thing from my mind. Under Dr. Cox's caring tutelage, however, that's exactly what happened. My confidence was renewed and my strength sustained. Even when my personal situation grew so stressful that I fled work and home during summer break from school for a much needed sabbatical, Dr. Cox spent countless hours on the phone with me, walking me through the analysis of my collected data, stepping me through the process of generating statistically significant findings, guiding me through the reporting of my conclusions, and helping me pull it together into a finished package.

What could have been one of the most horrific periods of my life was instead a time that I will always reflect on fondly. Had I not successfully completed that research project—a requirement for graduation from the Master's program—it would have only added to the failure and despair that sought to destroy me during that period. Dr. Cox connected with me and as a result was instrumental in saving my life.

Tom Bird is a successful author and teacher who believes in his students. He believes in them sight unseen. He believes in them from the moment they step into his classroom . . . before he even knows their name or what sort of book they're attempting to write. He believes in his students for one simple reason. Tom believes we're all divinely led. Call it a higher power, God, the universe, whatever name you are comfortable with. Tom believes with every fiber of his being that each individual has that spirit within them— that small, still voice—which is intended to guide us through each day of our continual journey toward our own unique purpose.

"The decision to be a teacher was made for me," Tom explains. "I've been given a great opportunity to share with others something they need to know."

Tom believes in the potential of his students because they have been led to him . . . led to him to have the opportunity to benefit from the knowledge, skills, and abilities that he has been given to share with them.

Because Tom believes in the students, his approach is not focused on results, but on the process of offering what he has for them in the most compelling way possible.

"I'm a perfectionist," Tom proclaims. "I choose to be the best I can be and give everything I have to all that I take on."

Tom gives teaching his all because he believes the greatest tragedy in life is that some people die without ever being who they were meant to be . . . to live life. As a result, he is invigorated in his mission to give each student that opportunity, despite the long, cramped plane flights, dreary hotel rooms, and lonely hours alone. Tom is intrigued by the process whereby a person comes to know who they are truly meant to be.

Tom describes how the process unfolds. "At the beginning, I have all the energy in the classroom. But soon the hunger that drove them to me causes them to become open. The students become aggressive in their quest to learn all they can."

He recounts a time when on a break a woman with a burning question blindly followed him right up to the urinal in the men's room. Tom smiles when he describes these unusual situations.

"I'm not upset by that kind of behavior. It's exciting to be around. I find these people so interesting who are doing something to become who they are meant to be rather than just talking about it. Their energy feeds me," Tom said, as he explained his unconditional approach.

In the end, Tom has the satisfaction of knowing he did the best he could. He knows that each student will choose what they learn from the experience. True, Tom is teaching classes designed to help struggling authors write and publish their work.

"But, if a person just comes to know themselves more or to do something entirely different with the information I've given them, that's okay too," Tom claims.

Tom believes in each individual in his class. I felt it from the moment he began to talk. Having floundered as a writer for years, compensating by telling everyone it was just a hobby, I had secretly known that this was part of what I am supposed to be doing with my life. Yet every attempt to learn the ropes had been met with discouragement. The messages I kept receiving from others told me that I was a fool with an impossible pipe dream. These messages, both overt and covert, crushed my spirit so completely that I would sometimes go for months without writing a word, only to finally succumb again to the flood that gushed from within.

I became embarrassed about it, and I built walls around my feelings to protect me from more hurt. I gave up on writing ever being more than a hobby or an ability I applied in the business world. I forced myself to believe that real authors lived on a higher plane than I could ever reach, so I would not even consider it a possibility. Being a coward was safer.

I only went to Tom's class at the urging of a friend. I didn't expect to learn anything. Then Tom opened his mouth and said, "I may die a fool, but I won't die a coward."

I was at once converted, as he continued throughout the weekend to urge us to believe we could achieve our dreams. By the end of his workshop, the fire was kindled brightly inside me.

Tom did that. His belief in me, without knowing a thing about me—not even my name—without ever reading a word I had written . . . that is what opened my mind and my heart to receive the divine message delivered perfectly through Tom.

Part II: How Does Teaching Common Sense Work?

The day will come when after harnessing space, the winds, the tides and gravitation, we shall harness for God the energies of love. And on that day, for the second time in the history of the world, we shall have discovered fire.

– Tielbard de Chardin

The Seven Commonsense Principles of Effective Teaching

Common sense is the knack of seeing things as they are,
and doing things as they ought to be done.

— Calvin Ellis Stowe

Three

From the wonderful examples of all my great formal and informal teachers, I've learned what it takes to be a really good teacher. Moreover, I realize how much they enriched my life, and thus how critical it is to all humanity that each of us be a good teacher. I've tried to emulate their example and want you to learn from them too. We all can and will benefit from the lessons of the good teachers we've had, if we only allow ourselves to be open to receive those lessons.

To begin the lesson and introduce the principles I've derived from my life lessons, recall the earlier definition of a principle. Principles are inarguable truths about our human existence, with principles of science—such as gravity—being the most commonly understood. Principles operate in the world, whether we are conscious of them or not, and how we interact with them generates a continual stream of positive and negative consequences in our lives.

I refer to the lessons I've learned from my great teachers as *commonsense principles* because of how they were revealed to me—how I was made conscious of these principles—through my interactions over time. Webster defines common sense as the *sound and prudent* but often unsophisticated judgment of ordinary people. Common sense is the knowledge formed from everyday life experience . . . experiences like those I described with the teachers I've known. At this stage in my life, I have also been exposed to all the sophisticated concepts about teaching in the Adult Education Master's program.

After reflecting on it all, I've come to the *sound and prudent* conclusion that every commonsense thing I've learned in everyday life, and every sophisticated thing I learned about teaching, all point to these seven commonsense principles for being an effective teacher: be committed to a vision, give unconditional love and acceptance, make a connection, be inspiring, be structured and organized, be a good coach and lifelong learner, and believe in others. Helping others learn and grow is best accomplished by a combination of these seven behaviors exhibited to me by my great teachers. In fact, together they are critical to facilitating learning and growth. Let's look at each one of the seven.

Principle #1: Be committed to a vision.

Lynn Whipple was able to teach me life-changing lessons, despite how things *were*, because he was committed to a vision of how things *could be*. His focus and determination in that regard were unwavering. It was his relentless passion that finally dissolved our resistance, shattered our outdated paradigms, and made us open to learn from him. I was reminded of Lynn when I learned about Myles Horton.

Men do less than they ought, unless they do all that they can.
– Thomas Carlyle

From a young age Myles Horton recognized his life vision of helping others improve their lives and ultimately popularized the use of education as a means to transform society. Growing up in the rural south, Horton's philosophy, educational theories, and values have deep roots in his southern rural experiences. He believed that God is love; therefore, you love your neighbors. You love everyone equally with no discrimination. Horton also felt that people have the ability within to learn to solve their own problems together. He believed that he was here to help people do that, no matter the cost. Horton dedicated his life to helping others.

Horton claimed you are "supposed to serve your fellowmen . . . education is meant to help you do something for others." He was an advocate of education for action and, because of its focus, it was dangerous education at times.

During his lifetime of dedication to his vision, Horton was threatened with arrests, beatings, even death. He watched colleagues assassinated, was investigated by the government, falsely labeled as a Communist, and had his school run out of two different towns. Through it all, Myles Horton remained committed to his vision.

Before his death in 1990, Horton wrote the following about his motivation and dedication. "Christ is one of the few examples of someone who simply did what he believed in and paid the price . . . . When he was told, 'You can't do this anymore; we're going to kill you,' he kept on doing it. I learned from Jesus the risks you've got to take if you're going to act. To make life worth living you have to believe in those things that will bring about justice in society and be willing to die for them."

Demonstrating commitment to a vision requires that you're clear in your own mind about your core beliefs and values, that you have a vision for your own life, that you see the connection between your life vision and the vision for all humanity, and that you're actually pursuing the fulfillment of both.

There's a fine line between being clear about a life vision and developing a limiting sense of identity. In the business world, we refer to the vision that we have for our company as the ultimate—the virtually unachievable ideal—toward which we're ever yearning and striving. Our vision is our perpetual motivation to improve. It's our compass for the journey.

Commitment to a life vision requires that you be a good student, always learning and growing, never getting stuck in an outdated paradigm, but constantly evolving your own sense of identity, consistently moving ever closer to the person you were born to be.

Being the kind of teacher others will follow into the light of a brighter day requires persistence in the face of all resistance, the energy for which can only be supplied by the vision of something worth fighting for.

Teaching those in our circle of influence is a commitment. Demonstrate for others an unwavering commitment to your teachable point of view, which is based on a vision that is greater than ourselves, and they will follow you through learning and growth.

Principle #2: Give unconditional love and acceptance

It's the thought that counts. This old saying teaches the importance of recognizing the effort, which is closely tied to the theory of positive reinforcement. That theory is based on reinforcing or recognizing what someone did well, even if all you can find to recognize is the attempt. Positive reinforcement of behavior that you want to encourage someone to continue has been shown much more effective than stressing everything they did wrong or that which you want them to stop doing.

In the same manner, if I want to encourage someone to learn and grow, then I will be the most successful by finding something positive on which

> The teacher who walks in the shadow of the temple, among his followers, gives not of his wisdom but rather of his faith and his lovingness.
> —Kahlil Gibran

to focus. That's what giving unconditional love and acceptance is about. It's about accepting others as they are—even if you do not understand them—and actively seeking out their positive qualities and attributes . . . that part of them that you can reinforce and on which they can build.

Mrs. Black, my piano teacher, and Gordon Inscore, my neighborhood grocer, were prime examples of this principle. Their ability to make each and every individual feel special and valuable melted many hardened exteriors and fears, and created an opening for learning to occur.

You can't teach by alienating those you are trying to teach. Helping others learn and grow requires that you demonstrate unconditional love and acceptance.

Being able to demonstrate love and acceptance for others requires that you first love and accept yourself. You have to be comfortable and secure in your own skin. You can't give something that you don't have.

In order to reach that state of being—the place where you love and accept yourself and thus can give that love and acceptance to others—you must be a good student. That means always mining your subconscious, always attending to your own psychosocial development, always growing into your one true self . . . the self you love and accept.

It is then that this love and acceptance of others can flow out of you like a mighty river, flooding the lives of all those around you.

Demonstrate unconditional love that transcends the human condition, respects individuals for who they are, and accepts them without reservation. Let this be one of your primary goals when interacting with others. Teach others out of this loving posture not because you know the topic or you crave the attention. Be a teacher because you care about others and are capable of acknowledging the uniqueness of each individual. Then and only then will you lessen their apprehension and defensiveness, so they can truly learn and grow.

Principle #3: Make a connection.

Each individual is different. Each possesses a special blend of talent, personality, and past experience that makes each unique. And each is experiencing some different life stage each time we encounter them. Making a connection with others requires an awareness of these facts as well as an unselfish abundance mentality . . . a genuine belief that there is more than enough success to go around, and others' success does not come at the expense of your own.

A man all wrapped up in himself makes a small bundle.
– Author Unknown

Making an enabling connection requires a genuine abundance mentality that drives an earnest desire to see others succeed. It requires you to be actively seeking how to best connect with others, in order to be instrumental in bringing about their success.

Cultivating this ability requires that you be a lifelong student of human nature, always seeking and learning to interpret those verbal and nonverbal cues that will lead to those connections with others. That is what Dr. Cox did with me. He connected with each of his diverse students as the unique individuals we are.

When Jesus walked upon the earth, he knew that we are all connected, and that by nurturing that connection with love and compassion, we lift each other up. Jesus connected with others where they were—in the streets, at the riverside, in the gardens, at the watering well—and created an ever-growing following. He embodied this heart of one who acts out of a desire to help others of which the Dalai Lama speaks: "Compassion is what makes our lives meaningful. It is the source of all lasting happiness and joy. And it is the foundation of a good heart, the heart of one who acts out of a desire to help others. Through kindness, justice toward others, we ensure our own benefit. There is no denying that if society suffers we ourselves suffer." Connecting with others requires that you have empathy for what they are experiencing. Forming a sincere connection with others is based upon this heartfelt understanding and compassion for their situation. Dissolving the barriers and building the necessary level of trust required to help lead others through learning and growth stems from a genuine, compassionate, empathetic heart.

Making a connection with someone requires an outward focus versus inward focus. It requires that you look at that person and really see them . . . not just what sits at the surface, but the real person underneath. You have to see their unique situation, not as you think it should be, rather as it feels for them.

Be a teacher who is capable of *being with* others in their own unique experience, not simply because you are a so-called expert. Caring about the subject matter you may be attempting to teach can never replace the personal connection between the teacher (the helper) and the student (the helpee).

Demonstrate empathy for others. Start with them from where they are. Genuinely care most about helping them get to where they are trying to go, using the subject at hand and the mechanics of teaching merely as one of the vehicles, and you will be instrumental in facilitating others' learning and growth.

Principle #4: Be inspiring

Mrs. Isbill inspired me to spread my wings and fly at a time when I needed it most in my young life. Then, just when I thought the mold of my life was set, Ken came along and put new wind beneath my wings. Both taught me the power of inspiration.

"Come to the edge," he said.
They said, "We are afraid."
"Come to the edge," he said.
They came. He pushed them,
and they flew.
– Guillaume Apollinaire

Nothing will ever be perfect. If we search for issues, problems, and roadblocks, plenty can certainly be found. But that pessimism serves no purpose in our battle to help each other learn and grow. Being an inspiration involves giving a healthy measure of respect to those problems that need to be defeated, while focusing a heavy majority of effort instead on the possibilities.

Being an inspiration to someone requires a stubborn refusal to let them underestimate themselves or to ever give up, regardless of their circumstances or the problems they face. Being an inspiration to others might mean that sometimes you are the only guiding light they can see in their present situation. So your enthusiasm must be sustained enough to carry you both through.

Being an inspiration to someone can be like holding up a magic mirror in front of them . . . one in which they see not their current perception of themselves, but the person you see them becoming . . . that one-of-a-kind, special person they are.

Being an inspiration to others requires that you believe in the possibilities, yourself, and the power to achieve them. It requires that you are fulfilling this continual stream of possibilities in your own life, so you can serve as a shining example to others. Being an inspiration requires that you be a student, constantly evolving and pushing the envelope.

Paint an inspiring picture of the possibilities that goes beyond contrived boundaries. Challenge paradigms in this nonthreatening way. Lovingly dissolve those mental models to help others see beyond the walls of their own metaphorical cave. Respect what is already in their cup and how it got there, while at the same time creating room for something new. Inspire a new hunger and thirst, and honor their freedom of choice, and you will have enabled their learning and growth.

Principle #5: Be structured and organized.

Regardless of where a person grows up in the world, from the earliest age of awareness they will find themselves within a common culture that organizes and structures their existence. It is the structure that organizes their lives as members of the society. That structure is made up of the socially transmitted and shared patterns of behavior, customs, attitudes, tacit codes, beliefs, values, arts, and knowledge that are uncritically formed and promoted through daily interaction and routine. This structure is perpetuated through folk tales, repetitive experiences, parental models, familiar occasions, and cultural events. Interestingly, within this framework, great

Work joyfully and peacefully, knowing that right thoughts and right efforts inevitably bring about right results.
—James Allen

creativity, innovation, and invention occur. The cultural framework provides for the basic human left-brain need for security, so that the right brain can have the freedom to explore greater, more creative endeavors.

The explanation lies in the fundamental nature of human society and the link with how the human brain functions. Humans have a physiological need for this secure structure even in learning endeavors. They expect it. Without it, they would become consumed by the need to create it. Before we can be inspired to work for something new, we need the basic assurance that the framework is in place . . . the structure is sound . . . thus preventing us from thinking this learning event may be a waste of time. Recognize and accept that conditions in the learning environment will never be predictable and perfect. Exceptions will be the norm. Prepare for this in advance by employing an organizational system and structure that provides a framework for quick response and improvisation.

The application of this structure is evident in my real-life examples of the factory, where I began my career, in the Apollo 13 story, and in Coach Erwin's coaching methods for molding us into good student-athletes. However, it can be a little less intuitive in more informal teaching environments. Here are some informal examples.

If you are a manager with a new employee you want to teach to perform in his or her new role, you need a structured way of delivering the necessary instruction and coaching. Employees, especially new employees, need regular, specific, actionable feedback, if they are to perform to the best of their capability in the job. Haphazard, inconsistent, negative, or vague feedback or instruction will not be successful in helping employees learn and grow.

The same is true if we're talking about teaching your children or helping a friend. If you allow your child or friend to repeatedly engage in destructive behavior without saying a word, then you suddenly decide one day to say or do something about it, this sudden act, lacking consistency and not grounded in a foundation of teaching and example-setting, would either seem shocking or inconsequential to them.

Being structured and organized in your attempts to mentor others and model learning, as well as sharing your proven learning and growth methods with others, is part of what makes you a good teacher, role model, and inspiration. It requires that you possess a structured approach for attending to your own personal learning and growth. It requires that you are a good student.

Model a structured and organized approach in your efforts to help others, which is focused on the goal of fulfillment of potential, while being flexible enough to appreciate the process of learning and growth. Plan and organize around this flexible framework within which creativity can flourish. Apply a facilitative structure to your teaching efforts and you will be providing a safe environment in which others can relax and explore their learning and growth.

Principle #6: Be a coach and lifelong learner.

My first basketball coach, Wayne Erwin, taught me what it means to be a coach. Since that first experience with him, I have gone on to have other good coaches in my athletic endeavors and have learned from each of them that coaching involves role modeling. A good coach sets the standard and then mentors others in their attempt to meet that standard.

The leader who exercises power with honor will work from the inside out, starting with himself.
—Blaine Lee

It's a different form of inspiration . . . one that not only inspires you to overcome challenges and achieve more, but also shows you the way. A good coach doesn't ask you to behave on the athletic field in a manner that will bring honor to the school, yet fails to behave in an honorable manner themselves. A good coach models that desirable behavior and provides the necessary mentoring and correction to help others do the same.

Good coaches are able to continually set new and higher challenges and then model the way forward, because they themselves are always learning and growing too. When a coaching system is established, all team members, including the coach, share learning. Something reciprocal occurs.

Listen to the interview of a coach whose team has just won a major championship and you will hear it described in his or her comments. Even if he or she is a seasoned coach with many years of experience, previous teams, and prior championships, they will speak of what they learned from this team . . . this season . . . this championship. It happens without fail. Being a good coach promotes and teaches coaches and players alike how to engage in lifelong learning.

If you want to coach someone, to help them learn and grow and fulfill their purpose, you must model that same pursuit of learning and growth. If you want to help them with lifelong learning, then you must be a lifelong learner yourself. You shouldn't expect to lead someone where you are not willing to go.

Being a good teacher requires that you be a good coach and role model. Being a good coach and role model requires that you be a lifelong learner . . . a good student.

Be a role model that sets the learning and growth standard for others. Take pride in what you do, if you expect those in your circle of influence to adopt the same sense of pride. Demonstrate the level of effort required to be all that they were born to be, by attending to your own lifelong psychosocial development while nurturing theirs.

Help those around you discover that nothing worth having is without effort, not even knowledge, understanding, skill, and self-actualization. Create in others the desire to set stretch goals throughout their lives and to work to reach them, and you will have set the standard for continual learning and growth.

Principle #7: Believe in others.

Tom and Ken's belief in my ability to write and create compelling stories is not what made me a creative writer. Their belief in me to do more than I had previously allowed myself to do, however, is what set that ability free. It's as if they reached inside me to a place that I didn't even know existed—buried deep in my unconscious mind—and found a hidden treasure. It was there all the time. But they had the wisdom and courage to lead me to it.

No man can reveal to you aught but that which already lies half asleep in the dawning of your knowledge. If he is indeed wise he does not bid you enter the house of his wisdom, but rather leads you to the threshold of your own mind.
– Kahlil Gibran

That's what believing in others is all about. It's about a confidence that treasures are hidden inside each individual, just as you possess your own unique treasures. You don't need to be jealous or intimidated or covetous of their treasures. Blended together our individual talents complement one another and combine to lift us all higher. The joy of doing what we were born to do emits an energy that feeds all of us. Believing in others is about realizing that we are all wonderfully endowed creatures connected by a common energy that joins us in this common pursuit of our one true self.

Believing in others requires an understanding that we are in each others' lives for a reason. It requires a belief that life is not about what you can get, but about what you can give. Tom and Ken have shown me that in giving we generate exponentially more energy than we could ever gain otherwise. When you allow your energy and belief to flow into others, they burst into flight, and they take you along for that exhilarating ride.

Be a teacher who is governed by a positive, "Yes, you can!" attitude toward others. Know that individuals are being led on their own unique journey to self-actualization, and you are meant to be instrumental in that quest. Respect their ability and their right to choose. Trust them and simply give them the absolute best that you have to give. Realize that their ultimate enlightenment will not come from you, but from within themselves. Your expertise and experience is simply the vehicle to facilitate their journey. Understand these principles and let them be your guide, and you will be one who helps others release their unique inner genius.

The Seven Commonsense Principles Are Interdependent.

These seven commonsense principles are the sound and prudent conclusions drawn from my profound everyday life experiences. Be inspiring. Be a good coach and lifelong learner. Give unconditional love and acceptance. Be committed to a vision. Be structured and organized. Make a connection. Believe in others.

Leading others through the fog and into the light of their own self-realization is no easy task. Each individual teacher possesses a myriad of talents, skills, and experiences, while each individual learner has an equally overwhelming number of factors at work inside of him or her.

Each individual—teacher and learner alike—is likely to be in different developmental life stages, some predictable, some not so predictable, when they encounter one another. Each has his or her own perceptual learning style as well as cognitive style. People have various forms of intelligence that can't be gauged with a mere standardized test. Individuals have diverse motivations driving them. Each has been exposed to a unique personal history and somewhat unique culture and social environment, which result in each having a particular personality. All these factors work together to make it difficult for us to consistently and successfully practice the recommended teaching behaviors, while at the same time causing us as learners to find it equally challenging to respond positively to learning opportunities.

This statement from an unknown source sums up the resulting interaction. "We're often surprised that we fail to communicate, when we ought to be surprised that we ever really do communicate. It's that difficult."

That's why these seven principles are so critical. They create the foundation for a relationship between us as individuals that can facilitate and enable learning. The way to achieve this facilitative relationship is to practice these seven principles religiously.

All too often the misperception exists that being a subject matter expert makes one a good helper or teacher for others. While knowledge and experience can make one a better teacher, the truth is content knowledge and experience alone are not enough to challenge the learners' old assumptions, break down barriers, build trust, and facilitate the resolution of conflicts inside the individual who is wrestling with his or her own paradigm shifts and developmental growth.

Another misperception also prevails that teaching is a profession and reserved only for those who have a mastery of the mechanics of teaching. Methods for assessing training needs, tools for course design, alternative approaches to training development, different mediums and styles of content delivery, and techniques for course evaluation and learner testing dominate that paradigm. While this facilitative, enabling structure and organization is important, it alone is not enough.

We all know this to be true, because we have had experiences with courses designed and delivered purely from this mechanistic paradigm. Recently, I enrolled in a one-day, noncredit personal development course at the local university. The instructor knew her subject and was very organized. So organized in fact that she had typed out every word that she intended to say. She said every word of it, too, much to my chagrin, as she sat at the end of the table, head down, eyes glued to the paper, monotone voice, stumbling occasionally over typos or inappropriately worded sentences, even stopping to correct misspelled words, reading to us the content of her manuscript.

She was structured too. She had thought about the left brain's need to have an opportunity to process facts and figures and the right brain's need to creatively explore the information. Thus she had carefully planned an equal amount of lecture and meditation time. She had even planned ahead and thought of meditative music for the soul and coffee and cake to feed the body. Despite my immediate shock at her overly scripted structure, I wanted to show my appreciation for her efforts by being the first to break the icy stiffness she had unwittingly created in the room.

I didn't even make it to the cake. When I started to pour my coffee, she was startled from her reading. Stopped in mid-pour, I was informed that it wasn't time yet for coffee and cake. I suppose we hadn't reached that point in the script yet. I returned sheepishly to my seat, only to listen to her read two more short paragraphs—lasting all of two minutes—after which she proclaimed, "*Now*, it's time to have coffee and cake."

We sat paralyzed through this all day, like children sentenced to sit in the corner. We ate, went to the restroom, or meditated when the script said it was time. When the script said it was time for questions or discussion, prompting her to solicit us, we were too numb to even produce anything. The overdependence on her very knowledgeable, organized, inflexible structure wasted an opportunity to explore a topic that might otherwise have been very valuable to me.

Determined not to come away feeling that I had thrown away my time and money, I persevered to walk away with some meaningful tidbit of learning. Mostly what I walked away with was the realization that being structured and organized is simply not enough. As in all things, taken to its extreme, this strength can become a huge weakness.

Another of the seven principles on which an overreliance sometimes develops is to be inspiring. The world is full of people who are totally focused on this principle. We refer to the successful ones as motivational speakers. They have mastered the art of speechwriting and public speaking. Some even achieve great wealth and notoriety as a result of their ability to give a stirring address. Down through history this talent has been applied in many fields where oratory is the primary, if not the only, responsibility. Preachers and politicians have probably been applying this talent the longest with the public speaker for hire and the infomercial-type motivator arriving on the scene with the television age.

There is absolutely nothing wrong with a focus on being an inspiring, motivational speaker. Do not call yourself a teacher, however, simply because you can deliver a moving public address. Motivational speakers should instead be called exciting speakers, because that is what they do. They excite their audience. Emotions are stirred. A whole range of emotions may be experienced while listening to the exciting speaker. People may laugh, cry, and feel shame, regret, or desire. They may even feel compelled to take action. They may purchase the book or product most closely associated with the exciting speaker. They may even promise themselves and God to change something in their lives, to right some wrong, or to develop some new habit. The next morning, nonetheless, when they awake with some distance now placed between the exciting moment and the present, they find that the excitement is not nearly as strong anymore. They may find it completely gone and may even feel foolish about their reaction while in that excited state.

Emotions are easy to stir. They sit just beneath the surface poised and waiting for that stimulus. The emotional response occurs quickly. A good speaker will put that emotion grabber right at the beginning for that very reason, to elicit that immediate emotional response that will draw the listener in for the thirty or sixty minutes they are speaking. If the exciting speaker can hold the audience's attention for that period of time, they have done their job.

Motivation is something entirely different. If I'm a teacher, I certainly need to motivate my students. I need to motivate them to explore, study, learn, and internalize the material. I need to motivate them to transfer the learning to their own situation. I need to motivate them to make the new knowledge and skill a permanent part of their repertoire.

Teaching is about more than just stirring the emotions. Learning and growth occurs on a much deeper level, especially in adults who have such entrenched patterns and habits—those mental models—that place almost impenetrable boundaries on their thinking.

The truth of the matter is that I can't motivate anyone to learn and grow. What I can do, as a teacher, is work to find the demotivators that are creating those false boundaries and strive to help expose and eliminate as many of those as possible.

That's what effective helping and teaching is all about. It requires all seven principles. Being inspiring is very important. But it's only one of the seven. Stirring the emotions is certainly a good beginning, but it is only that . . . the beginning. This relationship between all seven principles can be depicted as a living organism. *(Refer to Figure 1.)*

From those earlier examples of the structured teacher and the exciting speaker, we can begin to see that all seven factors, functioning in concert, are critical to success. Under further exploration, we can illustrate how interrelated and mutually dependent on one another they actually are.

Say, for example, I attempted to make a connection with you without truly feeling unconditional love and acceptance of you. My attempt would not be genuine and you would sense that in our interactions. The level of trust required for a connection to be established would be impossible under those conditions.

Similarly, making a genuine connection is necessary if I hope to be a good coach and instill a sense of pride and good work ethic. Individuals find their own source of pride. In my example of the basketball team, some were proud of the facelift we helped give to our gym. Some were proud of the amount of money they raised. Others were proud of how

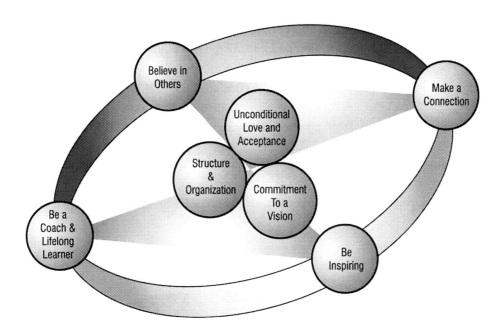

Figure 1: Seven Commonsense Principles of Effective Teaching

much their individual basketball skills improved. Still others found pride in the way the team gelled and the team spirit that developed. No doubt all were proud of the winning record we produced. The point is there were as many sources of pride as there were varying degrees of innate work ethic among the team members. Instilling a heartfelt sense of pride in accomplishment that is strong enough to justify and even in some cases improve that work ethic requires connecting with the students so that you know these important personal details. Making that connection with others shows respect for their uniqueness and empathy for where they are.

The Three Core Principles

If we continue to explore the mutually dependent nature of these critical principles, we begin to see that three of the seven are fundamental prerequisites to the other four, which is why they are depicted at the core of the organism. The three core fundamental principles, depicted as a cluster in the nucleus of the seven principles organism, are: give unconditional love and acceptance, be committed to a vision, and be structured and organized.

This chapter has already presented the fundamental nature of giving unconditional love and acceptance. Let's continue our exploration of that relationship by focusing on the other two factors represented in the nucleus—commitment to a vision, and structure and organization.

Consider the relationship between believing in others and commitment to a vision. *(Refer to Figure 2.)*

To truly believe in someone, I must be committed to a vision. If I don't believe with

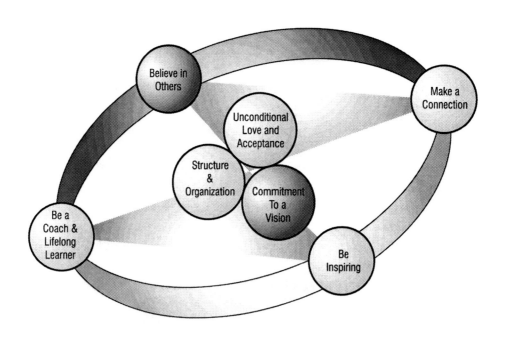

Figure 2: Mutual Dependence between Commitment to a Vision and Believing in Others

all my heart that I have a special purpose in this life, then why would I believe that any of my fellow humans do? How could I believe that my students do? Conversely, if I believe in and am committed to my life vision, then I'm capable of believing there is an equally compelling purpose for others' lives too. The commitment to a vision in which everyone can reach self-actualization and fulfillment of a unique purpose is fundamental to genuinely believing in the students and making a connection with them.

Likewise, being a good coach and lifelong learner also requires this compelling commitment to a vision. *(Refer to Figure 3.)*

Take Coach Erwin's example again. His was no easy task. He put in long extra hours, went far beyond what most would have described as his duty, and invested far more than his meager teacher's salary could compensate. Being a good coach requires being a role

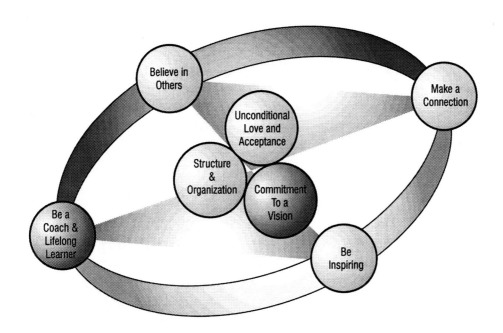

Figure 3: Mutual Dependence between Commitment to a Vision and
Being a Coach and Lifelong Learner

model. It demands that you set the standard . . . to never ask more of others than you would be willing to give yourself.

Instilling pride and a good work ethic and leading others to become lifelong learners is hard work. It's not something you do for money. Coach Erwin never got rich. It's not something you do for fame. Few people beyond our small community ever heard of our great accomplishments. Who would work that hard and expend that much effort—investing so much of themselves, sometimes even doing something unpopular at the moment—if they weren't committed to a vision that goes beyond personal reward and recognition? The two are mutually dependent. If you're committed to a vision, you'll not only expend the effort to be that role model, you won't be able to stop yourself. In the end it will be your continued commitment that is the motivational factor in influencing your students to truly learn and grow.

Being structured and organized may seem like the oddball of the three core elements, but it is equally fundamental to being an effective teacher. Our left brain needs the reassurance of some semblance of structure. Before I can allow you to coach me to learn and grow, for instance, I need the reassurance that there is some safety net if my attempt at something new fails. I need specific instructions and concrete feedback. This need for reassurance and security found in all humans is what makes being structured and organized a fundamental principle of being a good teacher. Structure and organization is a fundamental factor because it addresses a basic human need for security.

Let's continue to explore that point by looking at the relationship between being structured and organized and being a good coach. Given that part of our objective as a good coach is to instill a lifelong learning ethic applied toward personal growth, our fundamental structured and organized approach to helping the learner models that work ethic. It is the example of the organized, *intentional* pursuit of relentless learning and self-actualization that you are attempting to motivate.

Unlike the cultural norms, which are formed uncritically—without thinking, but simply through social conditioning—this learning and growth work ethic is something you teach the students to engage in critically. I want to be a good coach and to instill pride and a learning work ethic because I want my students to explore the possibilities, understand the options, and take action that moves them closer to being all that they can be. I don't have the answers. But I do want to work to help the students find their own answers, so as a coach I try to create the structure within which they can do that.

I go back to my country life on the farm for a simple analogy that demonstrates why these seven principles are interdependent and critical to the teacher's success.

On the farm we had a garden where we raised the fresh vegetables that graced our summer table, much to my culinary delight. My favorite of all the garden produce was the tomatoes. We raised all different kinds of tomatoes. Huge, red, juicy beefsteak tomatoes, perfect for backyard-grilled hamburgers. Large, red, tangy tomatoes good for Momma's homemade tomato juice and sauces. Big, sweet, low-acid, yellow tomatoes, with red stripes extending like a starburst from the stem, that just melted in your mouth. Tiny, round, cherry tomatoes, which we called "tommy toes," that were good in salads or just for a quick snack. And small, oval-shaped, yellow tomatoes that we called pear tomatoes, which I loved to slice up with peanut butter on warm toast. Mmm-mmm, good! They were all different. Still, at their heart, they were all the same, and I loved them all.

Raising tomatoes, in fact raising anything in the garden, is fairly basic. To avoid the killing late frosts of a lingering winter, plants are usually started in covered, protective beds or indoors in a hothouse before transplanting outside. All that's really required is to plop the seed, usually saved from last year's crop, into a small container of dirt, add water regularly, place it in the sunshine, and protect the seedlings from cold, killing weather. Seed, soil, water, and sunlight. That's really all that's needed to grow tomatoes.

Even after the hothouse plants are transplanted to the garden, the basic formula remains the same . . . tomato plants, soil, water, and sunlight. However, I've learned the hard way on the farm that there's more to it that that. Those things are essential, no doubt, but they alone are not sufficient if I want to grow really great tomatoes . . . the best I can possibly grow.

The clue lies in comparing the untended garden to the tended one. If the tomato plants are left to fend for themselves, with just the occasional rain and sunlight to nourish them, they will bear fruit. As they become buried in the weeds that inevitably overtake the garden and entrenched in the hardened, sunbaked soil, however, their fruit becomes small, knobby imitations, dry and bitter, hard and tough-skinned, not at all the sweet, juicy fruit that I love.

Much more was required to grow the prizewinning tomatoes we enjoyed on the farm. Daddy worked the soil until it was as fine as powder, and he infused it with the natural fertilizer provided by the cows' previous winter spent in the barn. We regularly added fertilizer and irrigation to continually nourish our tomatoes. When the weeds began to invade our garden, we broke out the plow and the hoe to carefully cultivate the soil and remove each weed by its root to ensure it would not grow back. The soil was kept loose around the tender plants and lovingly cradled around the spindly base until the roots were firmly established and the plants were ready to stand on their own. When insects threatened to devour our plants or their fruit, all stops were pulled. Natural and synthetic remedies were employed to rid the garden of those invaders as we maintained a daily vigilance over our crop. Daddy provided continual support with trellises and similar homemade structures on which the vines could run and flourish, producing beautiful fruit safely protected from predators and the damp ground below on which the fruit would merely rot away.

If you asked my daddy how he grew so many different kinds of world-class tomatoes, he would describe not just one or two of those success factors, but all of them. It takes all of them, working together, regardless of which kind of tomato you are trying to grow.

By the same token, regardless of what topic you are trying to teach, regardless of what sort of individual you are trying to help learn and grow, it takes all of the seven commonsense principles, working together, to produce the best results. Knowing the subject matter may be essential, just as sun and water is to growing tomatoes. But subject matter knowledge alone is not sufficient.

Be inspiring. Be a good coach and lifelong learner. Give unconditional love and acceptance. Be committed to a vision. Make a connection. Be structured and organized. Believe in others. These are the seven principles of being a successful teacher. It's plain common sense.

How My
Good Teachers Did It

Whoever would be a teacher of men let him begin by teaching
himself before teaching others; let him teach by example before
teaching by word. For he who teaches himself and rectifies his
own ways is more deserving of respect and reverence than he who
would teach others and rectify their ways.

—Kahlil Gibran

Four

Some of my great teachers were not formal teachers at all. They were every day folks just like you and me. Here's what made them great.

Principle #1: Be Committed to a Vision

Lynn Whipple is clearly imbued with a vision of a world in which everyone's life has purpose—a purpose that can be carried out, even through the most regular, everyday activities of work or play—a world where we each enable one another to fulfill our unique purpose. Despite all obstacles, Lynn held to his vision as it began to infuse our team through his teachable point of view. Lynn was not a teacher in a school or educational setting. Lynn's conviction taught me, nonetheless, many valuable lessons.

Lynn reminds me of Myles Horton, who was instrumental in bringing about positive social change over a period of six decades in this country. Horton called his method a "two-eyed" theory of teaching, meaning he kept one eye on where people are and one eye on where they could be. Because of Horton's commitment to a vision of education as a catalyst for positive change, Horton's Highlander School helped many gain control of their lives both socially and economically.

Myles Horton and Lynn Whipple exemplify two teachers with a teachable point of view, never wavering, committed to a vision of adults learning and growing together. It's the vision of teachers like themselves that motivates and sustains them. It's their commitment that opens doors, opens hearts, and open minds. From Lynn Whipple and the life story of Myles Horton, I learned that commitment to a vision of adults learning and growing together to improve their lives is a catalyst for positive change.

To teachers like Myles Horton and Lynn Whipple, teaching is far more than just a job. It's far more than just subject matter expertise or good public speaking ability. To teachers like Lynn, who are committed to a vision, teaching is a way of life.

Far too many individuals end up in an educator role because they have been engaged in a certain type of work for a long time or because they have a knack for a certain subject. But they make no connection with the student. They lack the vision of people like Myles Horton and Lynn Whipple for how this educational experience can improve others' lives. The student is totally aware of this deficiency and describes it in their feedback as uncaring, insensitive, or out-of-touch teachers who don't listen, don't set clear objectives, and don't provide adequate feedback. Students who find themselves in these teachers' classrooms feel as if they are fighting through the educational process, gaining little to nothing from it, until it is reduced to a mere struggle to survive with a decent grade in the course.

This reduction of the education process to reading the teacher's mind, making the grade, and getting out as soon as possible is not an educational endeavor at all, but is all too often the norm. Having a measure of subject matter expertise and an ability to keep the process organized—understanding the mechanics of a well-run training program— may be important, but it is without question not sufficient to insure that the student truly learns something with which they can better themselves.

If struggling through these ineffectively run educational programs is our only hope for fulfilling our purpose in this life, then God help us. What's required is specialized attention that meets the unique needs of each individual, provided not just by those who chose teaching as a profession, but by all within our circle of influence. The motivation to provide that specialized attention stems from a deep-rooted and all-encompassing vision of how things could be for us all.

Principle #2: Give Unconditional Love & Acceptance

I learned from Mrs. Black because she embodied unconditional love and acceptance. James Redfield wrote about this kind of unconditional love in his book *The Celestine Vision*. It's a love that's based on a conscious existential awareness of the origins of life and our connectedness. This love never seeks to dominate or control its object. It's different from the human love with which we are accustomed that requires an object of focus—a parent, spouse, child, or friend. This unconditional love transcends all that, becoming a pervasive constant in our lives without an intended focus—freely offered to everyone and everything. It keeps all our other emotions in perspective, pervading our being so strongly that it leaves no room for conflicting emotions. We're capable of this pervasive, unconditional love when we're fully connected and open to its eternal source.

The Apostle Paul wrote about this love in one of his letters to the Corinthians in the New Testament of the Bible:

> *Love is patient. Love is kind. It does not envy, it does not boast, it is not proud. It is not rude, it is not self-seeking, it is not easily angered, it keeps no record of wrongs. Love does not delight in evil but rejoices with the truth. It always protects, always trusts, always hopes, always perseveres. Love never fails. (I Corinthians 13:4-8, NIV)*

This isn't the same as the unconditional love my mother freely gives me. It stands to reason she would feel this way toward me. She carried me in her womb and brought me into this world and from that moment has never wavered in her love and support.

In comparison, this love of which Redfield and Paul speak goes beyond such parental love. It involves complete and total acceptance of another person even if on the surface they appear to be different from us or their behavior seems entirely inexplicable. Acceptance is an expression through all actions and words that all individuals are valuable as persons. All forms of verbal and nonverbal language consistently communicate that they matter. It seems almost too obvious that genuine feeling and demonstration of this kind of respect would be critical to being an effective teacher.

When it comes right down to it, I may have learned a few things in my life by reading books, but almost everything I've learned has come from other people. I owe my continued learning and growth to not only the Mrs. Blacks and Gordon Inscores who have crossed my path, but to each and every individual. Mrs. Black and Go-Go taught me how to love and accept those individuals, so that whatever we might have to share with one another could pass between us. That was no small lesson.

Principle #3: Make a Connection

Myles Horton told the story of how he successfully ran the literacy programs on Johns Island. He observed the residents he wanted to help and paid attention to how they lived their lives. He realized they wouldn't trust or respond to an unknown and untested outsider. For Horton's work to be successful there, he knew he had to recruit trusted, influential members of this established community to train as teachers for his program. If Horton was to connect with these students, it would best be accomplished through others.

Like Horton, we must listen and be observant enough to quickly identify what will work in a given situation and be flexible enough to adapt as required. It's a customer service mentality that's often misunderstood and replaced with that of an egotistical tyrant boasting about what they know. Thankfully, Dr. Cox doesn't suffer from this misunderstanding. He recognized my situation. He tuned in to my feelings and needs. He connected with me and then proceeded to lead me to success.

It's not about how much we know. It's not about the teacher. It's about the student. To be an effective teacher, a connection must be established with those we are trying to help.

Myles Horton always said, "As an educator you have to start where people are, not from some abstraction or from where you are, or from where someone else is, because it's from where they are that their learning and growth will occur." He said, "If you have to make a choice between moving in the direction you want to move people, and working with them where they are, you must choose to work with them where they are." Dr. Cox exemplified this principle.

This approach of working with the learner where they are was popularized by a famous historical figure. A Jew named Jesus transformed modern-day religion when he walked upon the earth. Whether you believe, as Christians do, that Jesus is the son of God, there's no question that Jesus embodied this principle of working with common people where they were. Jesus' travels are documented in the New Testament books of the Bible. In a time when only certain high priests were deemed fit to gain access to God in intercession for others, Jesus took God to the people and challenged what the New Testament refers to as increasingly corrupt and self-serving leaders of the ancient church. He shocked his contemporaries by going into the wilderness, city streets, and even leper colonies to teach his message of love to people from all walks of life.

More important than this literal going to where people are, Jesus figuratively began his teaching moments from where an individual was through the use of parables. Known today in some circles as the great teacher, Jesus employed the use of stories, as did all the Jewish scholars or teachers of the day, according to William Barclay. Jesus popularized the concept beyond the Jewish community because it's grounded in the science of how the brain processes information as well as the science of how humans learn.

The brain most easily processes visual inputs. We may have difficulty understanding the concept of beauty, but if we see a beautiful baby, then we know what beauty is. Barclay explains that the parabolic approach or use of stories for teaching turns incomprehensible ideas or concepts into something concrete, something visual, that the brain can process. Moreover, this approach makes a connection with each unique individual learner by placing him or her inside the story and inside the learning experience. Jesus' parables would prompt the learner to pass judgment on something with which they were familiar then apply that judgment to a new or different situation. He connected with people on a personal level, starting a following that's still, centuries after his death, the largest in the world. If nothing else, this makes Jesus' approach to teaching notable. Jesus' teaching encouraged critical reflection, because he understood the undeniable principle of choice.

We have the ability and freedom to choose - good choices, bad choices, and every-thing in between. From the earliest ages of childhood, others may try to deny our freedom of choice, but the principle still operates in our hearts and minds. It's undeniable. Jesus understood that to enable adults to see and understand the learning points and to moti-vate them to choose to learn the lesson and apply it to their own life, he had to make a connection. Jesus did that through his parables. Dr. Cox does that through a genuine interest in and empathy for his students' well-being.

The humanist philosophy of teaching helps explain what makes a good teacher, what makes one capable of leading students to their personal, liberating awareness. It's about making a unique individual connection in order to discover the key to breaking the paradigms that are affecting every individual and have the power to literally prevent them from seeing new or unexpected revolutionary ideas. Some will have paradigms so hard-ened, after years of going unchallenged, that they literally can't see the rationale of any argument, regardless of how compelling it may be to others. Therefore, simply being a teacher who is a subject matter expert or one who runs an organized class will not be suffi-cient to facilitate learning and growth. In order to break through these boundaries, chal-lenge the learners' paradigms, and motivate them to choose to entertain new ideas, the teacher must connect with each student on an individual level.

People will choose whether they do or do not learn from others. Motivating them to learn requires establishing a unique connection with them. It's from where each indi-vidual is that his or her learning must occur. Jesus understood that. Dr. Cox understands it. From these life lessons I learned how important it is for a teacher to make a connec-tion with the student.

Principle #4: Be Inspiring

One of the ways Mrs. Isbill accomplished the feat of moving us beyond our narrow view of life was through the practice of what Paulo Freire called critical reflectivity and Jack Mezirow referred to as perspective transformation. The need to reflect critically in order to develop a more expansive perspective stems from our tendency to develop a limited view of the world around us. Regardless of what anyone else might say or do, we believe with great conviction that we are right. Like the cave dwellers who refused to loosen their bonds and leave the cave in Plato's allegory, it's human nature for us to cling to our version of reality.

This transformation is accomplished through the art of discourse, employed by Socrates, popularized by Plato, and elaborated upon by modern-day educators like Horton, Freire, and Mezirow. It involves exposing the narrow-mindedness we all will fall victim to in at least one area of our thinking. In a nonthreatening way, this method asks the learner to consider other possibilities. It does literally that. It asks. Socrates would pose questions to his fellow Athenians, listen, and ask more questions . . . always probing to the root of their assumptions. In this manner, Socrates led his students to challenge their own paradigms. He inspired them to see new possibilities. That's what Mrs. Isbill did for us. With her we talked ourselves right out of our own little cave and out into a world full of possibilities and hope.

Another important means by which Mrs. Isbill inspired us was her tireless willingness to lead us beyond our comfort zone . . . to actually be there beside us . . . to go with us.

I remember one of the talent shows that Mrs. Isbill organized at the school. My friends and I had won almost every year and, in this our final year at the school, were determined to win again.

Mrs. Isbill never played favorites and had worked during school and after hours to prepare each and every one of us for the competition. I didn't wish for anyone to perform poorly. I just hoped we would perform better than anyone else.

It was nerve-racking. There were people participating this year for the first time ever, so we didn't know what to expect. One in particular worried me, a lovely girl named Charlene who was a member of the school choir. I held my breath when it came her turn to perform. The music started, Charlene opened her mouth to sing, and immediately I heard it. From almost the first note, Charlene was off-key. She had started off on the wrong note, and although she was continuing bravely, she was hopelessly and noticeably off. My reaction immediately went from relief to sheer pain. I knew how much courage it took to stand alone in front of the entire student body and sing. I knew how mortifying this situation would be for anyone, especially someone like Charlene who was doing it for the first time. I literally hurt for her.

Then, there she was in a flash . . . Mrs. Isbill. She came sweeping out into the middle of the gym floor where Charlene stood alone on the verge of tears. "Stop the music. Stop the music," she said, waving her arms and never taking her eyes off Charlene. "Now, Charlene, you can do this. Just take a deep breath and start over." Mrs. Isbill held Charlene's attention with that characteristic regal gaze of hers. "Okay, start the music," she said, and when it was time for Charlene to begin, Mrs. Isbill sang the opening notes with her, directing her smoothly into the tune and timing of the song.

Mrs. Isbill stood there in front of her through that entire song, and Charlene never took her eyes off her. Charlene sang that whole song . . . on key . . . not for the bunch of snotty nosed kids in the gym. She sang it for Mrs. Isbill. Mrs. Isbill inspired her to do something that had seemed an impossibility only moments earlier. Mrs. Isbill inspired her, because she did it with her. That's what being an inspiration is about. It's not lip service. It's action.

I am who I am today because Mrs. Isbill felt obligated to inspire me. Somehow, she recognized that we were coming to her like full teacups, already running over the brim, filled up with ideas, assumptions, and beliefs about life. She knew there was no room in the cup to simply pour in more. First, she had to remove some of the old contents before we would be open to receive any new. That's what she did. She sat up there on that stool in front of our class, or stood in front of us when we were on stage, and she painstakingly dipped those old ideas from our cup, making room for the new and creating a thirst in us to fill that space. Then she put us on our own unique path out into the world with an openness and a confidence that defied our humble upbringing. Mrs. Isbill was inspiring, and that made all the difference.

Inspiring someone to act goes beyond motivation or exciting the emotions. Inspiring someone is a prerequisite to motivating and coaching them. Inspiration is about hope. They first must have faith that there is a reason to try something new and different.

Mrs. Isbill gave us that hope. She shared story after story of successes that originated right in our backyard. She paraded in front of us an endless stream of role models who had come from backgrounds just like ours. She organized one event after another to lead us out of our comfort zone and into exciting, uncharted territory. She helped us do what we had never even imagined. Mrs. Isbill made us believe it was possible. She was our reason to believe. That's what being an inspiration is all about. It's about hope.

Principle #5: Be Structured and Organized

Dr. Cindy Solomon taught me the instructional design (ISD) model for adult education. Having dedicated most of her adult life to the study, application, and teaching of curriculum development and instruction, Dr. Solomon knows all too well the importance of applying a structured and organized process to the endeavor of teaching adults. But what I learned in her class was only validating what I had learned from years of experience. Just as had been the case in the factory where I worked and at NASA, the ISD model and structured, well-designed lesson plans provide the framework within which the adult educator can maintain perspective on the mission and adapt as necessary to achieve it. The objectives and content of the mission may change from course to course or class to class—just as it did with the Apollo 13 flight—but the roles, responsibilities, and methods remain consistent. This fundamental consistency enables creativity to be unleashed in those with special knowledge, skills, or abilities to contribute.

I proved this for myself when I applied this model at my workplace. Once the framework was clear, my colleagues eagerly contributed to establishing meaningful objectives for the strategy under development, and more importantly, creative and fun techniques for achieving the objectives. Months later, one of those colleagues called me after he had joined another organization and was attempting to develop a training program there to introduce a new concept.

"Can you send me some information about that structured approach you used when we developed that training program together a few years ago?" he asked, and then continued. "I remember how much it enabled me to apply my creativity."

This gentleman was definitely one of the most insightful and creative people with whom I had ever collaborated. I needed no higher endorsement. Applying structure and organization is enabling. It's facilitative. It's not optional.

Even if the student's avenue of reaching fulfillment is in an art form, which might mistakenly be seen as a field demanding a lack of structure, structure and organization are equally important. For instance, when I began working with Tom as my writing coach, he provided structured, challenging exercises and specific targets on a daily basis. The exercises organized and focused my energy toward writing, calmed my nervous left brain, and released my artist within.

The commitment to a consistent system and process—a work ethic applied toward the productive acquisition of knowledge, development of skills, and enhancement of ability—is critical to perfecting one's craft and achieving one's purpose. It is the difference between just talking about something and actually doing it. Applying structure to coaching activities sets the example. There, structure provides the legitimacy to gain students' respect as a role model, to open them up to be inspired by your belief in them, and to allow an enabling connection to be established.

Principle #6: Be a Coach & Lifelong Learner

Coach Erwin's example provides the important lessons for being a coach and lifelong learner. He was able to be a successful role model to us for the reason that his title implies. He was successful because he coached. Unfortunately, coaches are too often portrayed as brainless buffoons . . . big jocks stuck in their glory days and not smart enough to do anything else for a living. Thankfully, we have compelling real-life examples to the contrary.

Paul "Bear" Bryant, legendary football coach at the University of Alabama, was one such example. According to those who studied Bryant's success, in public appearances, he promoted the typical coaching jargon of "select the right players; inspire them to win; and show them you care." However, when he was at work during practice, there was very little affection displayed, nor was there much in the way of lecturing or hollering. What Bryant did was exude the pride he expected from his players . . . and he watched and learned.

With video cameras stationed around the practice field, Bryant captured the idiosyncrasies of his players' movements in great detail and kept meticulous performance charts for every player. When he saw a player consistently making an error, he told him about it, walked him through the correct procedure, watched him do it right, and, yes, gave him a "Well done!" for mastery. Bryant's highly successful coaching method involved gathering data, providing feedback, questioning, informing and instructing, and rewarding, often simply with praise . . . certainly not the work of a dumb jock.

The research of an instructor at the University of Pennsylvania's Wharton School, Linda Richardson, defined the six critical factors for successful coaching.

The coach is a *role model*, living the desired behaviors. The coach is *trustworthy*, having earned the trust of the team members. The coach lets people figure things out for themselves, respects them and as a result is respected, creating the *mutual respect* necessary to coach someone. The coach is a good *communicator*. The coach draws upon his or her own related *experience* to help team members. The good coach provides positive reinforcement and *praise*.

From the writing of Peter Senge, Director of the Systems Thinking and Organizational Learning Program at MIT's Sloan School of Management, we can derive that coaches are leaders who not only model the desired behavior, but also provide "systems" that facilitate learning. Within these leader-oriented systems, learners are encouraged to take risks. Mistakes are both allowed and promoted as opportunities for learning. No blaming is allowed in this system that supports, recognizes, and rewards genuine effort. In these settings, the coach values the well-being of each individual, and as a result, learning occurs and is shared with all members of the team.

Learning, while stereotypically viewed as something that starts and stops at defined chronological ages, is in fact an ongoing lifelong process. It revolves around the realization that our learning and growth continues throughout our lifetime. Given healthy development of our identity, beliefs, values, and roles, we can more effectively affiliate with other people. This, then, makes lifelong learning and development crucial to being a successful teacher-coach and role model for others. It insures that our own psychosocial development reaches a level at which productive affiliation with other adult peer-learners is possible. Lifelong learning ensures that we are developmentally capable of exhibiting the coaching behaviors that are so crucial to facilitating the learning and growth of others.

Coach Erwin was someone who consistently taught me the importance of lifelong learning. In all that he modeled, it was clear that there was no acceptance of complacency or laziness—not from us or from himself. From Coach Erwin, I learned the pride of continual learning, growth, and improvement. From Coach Erwin, I learned the work ethic necessary to perpetuate that same positive learning and growth throughout the stages of my life. From Coach Erwin and others like him, I have learned that a good coach is not the one with all the answers. A good coach sets challenging developmental goals for himself or herself, as well as the students, and then proceeds to learn and grow right alongside them. When that exchange takes place it affirms the effort of both the teacher and the learner.

Principle #7: Believe in Others

"How do you know I can do this when you've never even seen any of my work?" I asked Tom after the workshop.

"I don't have to see your work," he replied. "I believe with all my heart that you were led to me because I could help you do what you're meant to do. That's all I need to know."

Tom believes in his students, even when they don't believe in themselves, and that makes all the difference.

Tom may be the teacher who made the difference for me, but he's certainly not the first to act out of a belief in the capacity and potential of others. Nor is he the first to follow divine leading in his quest to help others fulfill their potential. Martin Luther King, Jr. may be the most well-known *teacher* in recent days of this country to believe in people, despite overwhelming sentiment that his belief was futile.

King's 1963 "I Have a Dream" speech, delivered on the steps of the Lincoln Memorial during the African-American struggle for Civil Rights in the United States, clearly depicted a man committed to a vision. It and other of his speeches also reveal his belief in people to find the best within themselves. He didn't call for war, but for peace. He didn't preach division. On the contrary he talked of unity. He didn't cultivate hate, but rather love. He believed with every fiber of his being that each individual, black and white, contained the enlightenment within to make his dream a reality. King was right. It was his compelling belief in people to do the right thing that made the difference.

The answer to why this simple belief in people is so liberating and inspiring lies in the definition of what makes one an adult and the talents that make each person unique. Right away, it's easy to see that adults come not only in all shapes and sizes, but also possess unique combinations of talents. Tom's talents are apparent in his writing and teaching, as were Martin Luther King's in his speaking and leadership. Each individual is blessed with something they can do well, as a result of these talents that are hardwired into our brains.

The theories of critical reflectivity and perspective transformation of Paulo Freire and Jack Mezirow explain how adults apply these unique talents to learn from their experience. Critical reflectivity involves intentional evaluation of previous decisions, actions, results, and experiences with the goal of learning that transforms the learner's perspective and moves him or her toward positive learning and growth.

Humans learn from experience, either for better or worse, consciously or unconsciously. For instance, from all those who didn't believe I could be an author, I learned for the worse from that experience . . . that I couldn't fulfill my dreams. From these good and bad experiences, we learn and develop all kinds of limiting paradigms and mental models. By the same token, those experiences also result in the development of various forms of expertise and a unique identity.

For the individual to be enabled by the learning experience, to open up, to critically reflect on their situation, and to take the appropriate action, they need their unique experiences, expertise, identity, and talents to be respected. Just as Tom realizes that it's okay for his students to choose how they apply what they learn from him, people need the freedom to choose how they respond to what is being taught.

Believing that each person contains this enlightenment within is what makes Tom a great teacher. It's what makes it possible for him to break through to the students. It's also what creates the reciprocal learning opportunity. Truly valuing others leads not only to a desire to share our knowledge with them in order to help them learn and grow, it also leads to the recognition that they have something of value to offer to the interaction as well. It's this two-way exchange of energy that nourishes Tom and keeps him going mile after mile.

My Great Teachers Delivered Customer Service

The seven commonsense, teacher success principles, based on my studies and the experiences I've had with my great teachers, recognize the *customer service* aspect of helping others learn and grow.

In a formal sense, pedagogy, the education of the young, is characterized by the teacher knowing what the student needs to learn. It assumes, usually simply because of their young age, that the student's cup is not yet full. The teacher simply needs to pour in the contents that he or she deems important. Andragogy, the education of adults, on the other hand recognizes that the students enter the educational environment with a full cup. It recognizes that the adult student will choose how to rearrange the contents to make room for more.

Similarly, when a person calls a customer service hotline, they know what they want and need. It's the customer service representative's responsibility to respond to that need expressed by the caller. In this same manner, my great teachers demonstrated that same respect for me. The seven principles recognize that teaching is about helping others do whatever it is they want or need to do. Teaching is about providing a service to others. The seven commonsense principles work together to focus us on understanding and meeting those needs, and not on ourselves, or on our mastery of a particular topic.

My teachers understood my undeniable freedom of choice. Their teaching, characterized by the seven principles, was like handing me a new, larger cup. It still respected and honored all the contents of the old, smaller cup, which I could choose to keep or to discard. While at the same time, it created a thirst in me to begin to fill the new empty space with additional contents just as unique as I was as an individual.

These commonsense principles provide the means by which teachers can effectively challenge paradigms and open students to new possibilities. Teaching from this customer service perspective dissolves the barriers, removes the blinders, inspires the student, and leads them safely through that learning and growth process.

My Great Teachers Delivered Human Nourishment

The humanistic approach to adult education is rooted in the very science of human physiology and reason, which drives individuals toward their many daily choices. The teacher helps the learner apply their talents and learn their way through all the noise and confusion . . . all the good and bad experiences . . . all the paradigms to a place where they can make choices that will have positive consequences on their journey to reach their potential and to fulfill their purpose.

This idea of helping others reach self-actualization, whether applied from the perspective of psychology or education, is at the heart of being a teacher who believes in the student's ability to choose rightly . . . to filter the subject matter and to apply it to solve their own problems and improve their unique situation. The trick is in how the teacher exhibits this belief in the students.

Researchers Carkhuff and Berenson introduced what they referred to as the dimensions of human nourishment: respect, empathy, genuineness, and concreteness or specificity. "All helping and human relationships may be for better or for worse," they wrote. Delivering high levels of these four dimensions during the helping interaction ensures that the result will be for the better.

The helpee or learner has a much higher probability of moving through the growth phases of exploring, understanding, and acting, when these four helping behaviors are present.

Carkhuff and Berenson concluded from their fifteen-year research of all kinds of helpers, including therapists, nurses, teachers, and parents, that we're always delivering some level of these dimensions. If we think about it as a scale of degrees from one to ten, we are registering some point on the scale at all times. From the moment we open our eyes in the morning and begin to interact with those around us, with all our verbals and nonverbals we are delivering some level of these four dimensions, whether we are conscious of it or not. Most important, they found that the most successful helpers routinely exhibited high levels of all four of these dimensions.

Delivering high levels of the dimensions reduced defensiveness, broke through barriers, and built trust between the helper and the helpee . . . between the teacher and the student . . . between the parent and child. In that trusting environment, the student is safe to explore, learn, and grow . . . to choose to act in a way more likely to bring about positive natural results on their road to self-actualization. When we exhibit high levels of the dimensions of human nourishment, those around us are nourished emotionally and as a result are strengthened to begin to find resources within that they never realized they had.

Exhibiting genuine respect and empathy in all our interactions, characterized by concrete, meaningful communications, creates an atmosphere of trust. That trust provides a safe environment to calm the dinosaur left brain. It also allows others to retain their dignity.

An ineffective learning environment would be one in which low levels of the four dimensions are present and individuals are made to feel inadequate or incapable and are also made to feel that their previous experiences and accomplishments are of no value. Delivering high levels of the four dimensions, as my great teachers did, honors others, thereby removing many inhibitions about the learning environment.

We can show the link between the dimensions of human nourishment and the seven principles of teaching success. For instance, respect is the demonstration of my acceptance of you and my belief that you are valuable just as you are. It's not earned. Respect is freely given and deserved simply because you are my equal. In the learning setting, this nourishing dimension of respect, which is critical to the helping process, is demonstrated through the principles of unconditional love and acceptance and unwavering belief in others.

> Criticism has the power to do good when there is something that must be destroyed, dissolved, or reduced, but capable only of harm when there is something to be built.
> – Carl Jung

In comparison, empathy not only means respecting others, but also being able to be with them where they are. It's being able to see the world as they see it, understand what they are experiencing, and experience it with them without judgment. This important dimension of empathy is expressed in the learning environment when the teacher follows the principle of making a connection with the students, enabling the teacher to provide the specialized attention the students need.

Most importantly, genuineness is about being authentic in the helping relationship. It's the consistent representation on the outside of what is sincerely felt on the inside. As a teacher, unless my commitment to the vision is genuine, and unless I genuinely communicate respect and empathy to the student, I'll be unable to inspire or coach them. All seven principles must be delivered genuinely. When the teacher's commitment and motivation is genuine, the doors are opened to the possibilities.

Finally, concreteness is described as specificity. In a learning encounter, concreteness leads to elimination of the much-maligned vagueness in the helping process. The important dimension of concreteness is delivered in the helping process through the principle of having a structured and organized process facilitated by a caring instructor.

By delivering high levels of the dimensions of human nourishment through the seven commonsense principles, the learner is enabled to discover their own resources . . . their own enlightenment within. As a result, when the time comes to *go solo*, leaving the nest of the supportive teacher who has facilitated them through the learning process, they're enabled to incorporate the change and growth permanently into their lives.

My great teachers delivered consistently high levels of these dimensions of human nourishment and, as a result, awakened hidden treasures inside of me and forever changed my life.

Checklist for the Seven Commonsense Principles of Effective Teaching

Give Unconditional Love and Acceptance

- Focus on seeing the unique qualities and beauty in every person you meet. Intentionally make your first impression a positive one.

- Remember to smile. Be genuinely warm and open. Speak kindly and nonjudgmentally. Look for ways to affirm the other person versus tearing them down.

- Accept each person as they are. Force yourself, if necessary. Remember that every individual is the unique product of their own challenging experiences on life's journey. Look beyond a person's actions and focus on loving the soul of the person. Let this love radiate out to him or her through all your verbal and nonverbal communication.

- Respect each person's right to be who they are, feel what they feel, and think what they think. Remember that you don't have to compete with them, control them, or change them. Search for commonality versus difference.

Be Structured and Organized

- Remember that the dinosaur brain is naturally searching for safety and security and sometimes even creates feelings of panic. Accept that this is normal and okay, and that structure and organization are good for all situations.

- Satisfy the left brain's need for security by first and foremost attending to the method and approach taken in your words and actions. Give the other person's left brain a reason to trust what you are saying or demonstrating, by delivering the dimensions of human nourishment, by your orderly manner, and by your reference to analogous success stories, i.e., "You can trust me because this is what I have seen/done/heard . . ."

- Recognize that the left and right brain will always be fighting to take the lead. When interacting with others, expect this unpredictability. Don't judge others or form a negative impression for this reason. Stay flexible. Don't let their struggles between left and right brain cause you to deviate from your facilitative approach.

- Focus on creating an environment that enables the dinosaur left brain to rest and allows the creative right brain to soar.

Be Committed to a Vision

- Focus not on how things have been or how things are, but rather on how things could be. Be aware of your thoughts, feelings, hunches, and dreams related to those possibilities and act upon them whenever possible.

- Pay attention to the mysteries unfolding in each unique life. Be aware of all the dynamics that help and hinder that discovery. Focus on how you can assist by removing the barriers.

- Recognize that continual learning and growth toward our own unique fulfillment of purpose is the true nature of this existence, and likewise the reason for living. Therefore, be willing to go the distance. Put forth the effort, and do all that you can do.

- Remember to broaden your focus beyond yourself or those closest to you. Look beyond the surface of the human condition. Envision a better future that encompasses all creation and in so doing elevates the existence of every individual. Then work every day to make that vision a reality.

Be Inspiring

- Realize how difficult it is for humans to see beyond existing paradigms and mental models. Deliver a consistently high level of energy that defies logic and is sustained long enough for those hardened barriers to dissolve.

- Understand that everyone already has a full cup, and you can't simply pour in something new. Lead them through an exploration of the old contents and how they got there. Question the assumptions on which the desire to hold on to the old is based. Help them make the choice to let some of it go, so something new might take its place.

- Live by a "we can do it" attitude. Inspire them to take the first step into something new by taking that first step with them. Demonstrate that you're going on the journey with them.

- Paint a mental picture of the possibilities, and become a living reminder of those possibilities. Be their inspiration and guide—the wind beneath them—until they develop their own wings to fly.

Make a Connection

- Maintain an outward focus on others versus an inward focus on yourself. Give others your full attention.

- Look each person in the eye. Ask questions. Listen to what they are saying, as well as what they are not saying. Make it a priority to get to know them as individuals. Stay focused on those around you and the needs they are expressing both verbally and nonverbally.

- Focus on seeing the situation through the eyes of others. Don't project your feelings onto them. Rather, try to feel what they feel.

Start from where they are, not from where you think they should or could be.

- Remember that we're all connected by the same complex web of energy, so the energy you send into their life will come back multiplied into your own. Focus on how you can use your energy to lift each person you encounter.

Believe in Others

- Remove the words "no," "don't," and "can't," from your vocabulary. Replace them with an "anything is possible" attitude.

- Respect others' rights and abilities to make choices. Remember that each person is on their unique journey—a journey on which only they can choose their direction. Trust that you're playing your important part in that journey by simply believing in them.

- Realize that those you encounter possess the ability within to find the answers they need. Recognize that you're not the source of their enlightenment, but rather one of the tools to help them find it. Express your unwavering faith in their ability to be all they were born to be.

- Don't hold anything back. Ignore feelings of uncertainty, insecurity, or doubt, which the left brain continues to throw at you. Act on your intuition—the messages you're meant to deliver to others—and give each individual the most and absolute best you have to offer. Believe that this is a part of the reason you're here.

Be a Coach and Lifelong Learner

- Remember that others are watching. Attend to your own development and behavior. Don't just offer lip service. Model the standards you believe in. Support your words with action.

- Recognize that we're all engaged in lifelong psychosocial development. Create an environment in which every attempt at something new is an opportunity to learn. Focus on positive reinforcement for each attempt—failed or successful. Turn mistakes into growth and successes into rewards.

- Nurture a sense of pride not only from succeeding but also from the sheer act of trying. Find something to celebrate in each individual's effort.

- Remember that what you give to others creates a reciprocal relationship, returning multiplied to you, so that you're continuously learning and growing too.

Part III: How Can I Practice Teaching Common Sense?

Everybody can be great because anybody can serve.
You don't have to have a college degree to serve.
You don't have to make your subject and verb agree to serve.
You only need a heart full of grace.
A soul generated by love.

– Martin Luther King, Jr.

The Teacher You Already Are

When you are inspired by some great purpose,
all your thoughts break their bounds: your mind
transcends limitations, your consciousness
expands in every direction, and you find
yourself in a new, great and wonderful world.
Dormant forces, faculties and talents become alive,
and you discover yourself to be a greater person by far
than you ever dreamed yourself to be.

– Patanjali, 2nd Century B.C. Philosopher

Five

Do I have to say it again? We're all teaching someone something all the time. You may say, "Oh, not me. I'm just a housewife. I'm just a teenager. I'm just a banker." But, make no mistake, all kinds of people are watching you, interacting with you. And they're affected and influenced by that interaction. You're a teacher to someone who looks to you. We all teach someone whether we know it or not.

Many of the people from my life whom I've written about in this book, even those who were in formal teaching positions, have no idea the important lessons they taught me. This is especially true for those who didn't hold formal teaching roles. I was simply placed within their circle of influence at a time in my life when I was open to receive certain lessons that they were uniquely prepared to deliver.

Stephen Covey has popularized the concept of a circle of influence. Your circle of influence includes all those with whom you interact either formally or informally. You are a teacher to those in your circle of influence, depending on the situation, who's around, and what his or her need is. From this perspective, there are *teaching jobs* of all sizes. Sometimes you may be required to teach a really big lesson or maybe just a small one. You're still teaching even when it may seem insignificant to you. All are important.

This concept of teaching and learning from one another can be summed up by this poem, which has been circulated widely on the Internet and attributed to various known and unknown authors.

One of Life's Best Lessons

People come into your life for a reason, a season or a lifetime. When you figure out which it is you know exactly what to do. When someone is in your life for a reason, it is usually to meet a need you have expressed outwardly or inwardly. They have come to assist you through a difficulty, to provide you with guidance and support, to aid you physically, emotionally or spiritually. They may seem like a Godsend, and they are. They are there for the reason you need them to be. What we must realize is that our need has been met, our desire fulfilled. The prayers you sent up have been answered.

When people come into your life for a season, it is because your turn has come to share, grow or learn. They may bring you an experience of peace or make you laugh. They may teach you something you have never done. They usually give you an unbelievable amount of joy. Believe it! It is real!

Lifetime relationships teach you lifetime lessons; those things you must build upon in order to have a solid emotional foundation. Your job is to accept the lesson, love the people, and put what you have learned to use in all other relationships and areas of your life.

I'll bet you can think of someone who played this role for you. I'll even wager that, while reading this book you've remembered your own Mrs. Isbill, Mrs. Black, Go-Go, Lynn, Dr. Cox, Tom, and Ken.

Now turn it around. For whom have you played that role? Whom have you been teaching? Let's start by looking at your family. It's pretty easy to see how you're a teacher to your children. Almost every parent sees it as their place to teach their children important lessons. Some refer to it as a job, a responsibility, a chore, a burden, or an honor and a privilege. But almost all can agree it's a role parents play with their children.

What may not be so intuitive is the teacher-student role played with one's spouse. If you have a spouse, you certainly are teaching this person. I once heard a marriage counselor say to a spouse, "Every word that comes out of your mouth is either bringing the two of you closer together or pushing you farther apart." We may not like to think of ourselves as student or teacher when it comes to a spouse, but the fact remains. We're shaped by every interaction, either good or bad. We're teaching and learning, even with a spouse.

The same is true with extended family members. Siblings, cousins, aunts, uncles . . . if they're within the proximity of your circle of influence and you're interacting with them, then all are teaching and learning from one another.

Similarly, if you have or have had at any time in your life interaction with parents or guardians, they're learning from you. Oh, yes, you heard me right. Parents and guardians are learning from you. You may think they're not paying attention to you, but that time will come just like it does in every life when it will be their time to learn . . . even from their children.

I've heard it said that parents do not own their children. They help bring them into the world and teach them the things they need to get started. That's how it's supposed to work. But there comes a natural point at which the roles are reversed. The child emerges as the unique individual they were born to be, at which point they also become capable of delivering the important lessons others need to learn from them and through them . . . including their parents.

The situation at work is not that much different from the situation with family. In fact, we spend so much time with coworkers, both as a percentage of each day as well as a percentage of our lifetime, that they become a kind of family to us. Throughout our work lives associates take us under their wing, mentor us, teach us, and help further our skills and level of responsibility in our chosen field. Likewise, at one time or another, we befriend others and play the same role of mentor, teacher, helper, and supporter. Whether it be with our peers in the company, our managers and supervisors, or with our own employees, we're presented with many opportunities to teach in the workplace. We're teaching someone there something all the time, whether we're conscious and intentional about it or not.

What about outside of family and coworkers? We're exposed to people socially every day. It may be your oldest and dearest friend. It may be the new friend you've just made in your neighborhood. It may be the people you see at church. It may be your fellow members in your civic organization or club. It may be your butcher or your dry cleaner. It may be the girl behind the cash register at the convenience store where you stop for coffee each morning. It may be the complete stranger who bumps into you in the crowded shopping mall. If you stop to think about it, you're interacting with hundreds of people each week. And, yes, you're being both student and teacher during all those interactions. What kind of signals are you sending? How receptive are you to the signals you are receiving?

Finally, there's one last area where we need to look. That is at yourself. Even in those rare, quiet moments alone, you're teaching. You're teaching yourself. Your self-talk, your interaction with yourself, is a powerful teacher. If none of those other areas applied or mattered to you, this one surely does. So let's explore the teacher you already are in these situations with the following exercises.

Exercise 1

The purpose of this exercise is to become aware of the fact that you're already teaching others in your sphere of influence and what lessons you may be teaching them. Here are the directions for the exercise.

1. Read the scenario and think about the situation it describes. You may be able to think of a real example from your own life that is very similar.

2. Reflect on the scenario provided and on any similar real-life experience you've had. Ask yourself what you would think, feel, and/or do if you were actually in the situation described in the scenario. If you had a similar experience, think about what you did in that situation and the thoughts and feelings you had during that time.

3. Briefly describe, in the space provided after each scenario, how you would think, feel, and act in this situation. Or, if you have had a similar experience, describe what you actually did in that situation.

4. Don't write how you would like to behave, but how you actually think you would instinctively react to the situation. Remember, this is an exercise designed to make us conscious of good patterns that we would like to emphasize and not so good ones that we want to improve. So don't judge yourself. Just be honest with yourself.

Scenario 1:

You and your spouse have what could be characterized as an average marriage. You both have good jobs with a decent income that affords the regular vacations and material possessions typically associated with the good life. You feel fortunate to have an honest, hardworking spouse, and you're grateful for the good fortune that has been yours to enjoy. You have a very comfortable life.

Nevertheless, you sometimes feel a little unsatisfied. Occasionally, when your spouse spends more time working or engaged in his or her own leisurely pursuits, you feel irritated and unfulfilled. At times you even imagine yourself in a different job . . . a different life. You have to admit this life didn't turn out exactly the way you thought it would. But your spouse is good to you, and you have all the things a person could want or need.

✏ What would you think, feel, and do in this situation? Write your answer here.

_____

_____

_____

_____

_____

_____

_____

_____

_____

_____

_____

_____

_____

_____

_____

_____

Look at some of the possible reactions to this scenario. One option is that you try to make yourself feel guilty for being unsatisfied. You should learn to accept things as they are and be happy. Look how unfortunate some of the people around you are, you tell yourself. You should be ashamed for ever letting those desires cross your mind. You have more than enough to be fulfilled. So you try to will yourself to be complacent. Some things just are what they are, and we shouldn't question them, you convince yourself. Dreams are the foolish pastime of the young.

However, if you're committed to a vision, you realize that dreams and desires are the vehicle of the force that guides us ever closer to the person we were born to be . . . our one true self. A big deterrent to our self-actualization is the false sense of security that naturally results from a so-called comfortable life. If you choose to ignore those original or recurring dreams and urges—allow yourself to settle and become complacent—your journey stagnates. The person who's committed to their life's vision, even when they may not yet clearly see all that it entails, will search for ways to continue to learn and grow within the support structure provided by a sound relationship and financial situation.

If you wrote that you would seek to find a way to engage your spouse in the creation and pursuit of a common vision, capable of nurturing the self-actualization of both parties, then you are exhibiting the healthy behaviors that characterize the principle of commitment to a vision.

Scenario 2:

You've never had a doubt about how you wanted to raise your children. Your sense of what's right and wrong, good and bad, acceptable and unacceptable was engrained in you at a young age. You've expanded those beliefs a little in your adulthood, and you've worked diligently since your own children were born to teach them to be good people and upright citizens.

You practiced all your parenting skills on the oldest child, only to learn that it was never quite the same with the two children who followed. In fact, you have to admit that as you've watched them mature, none of them are turning out exactly the way you imagined they would. Sometimes their choices and behaviors even shock you. You just don't understand them anymore. They're not at all who you raised them to be.

✏ What would you think, feel, and do in this situation? Write your answer here.

_____

_____

_____

_____

_____

_____

_____

_____

_____

_____

_____

_____

_____

_____

_____

_____

_____

_____

One possible reaction is that you arrive at the obvious conclusion that they are children and you're the mature adult. Of course, that means you know things they can't yet even imagine. You have to be the parent. It's your place to tell them what to do, how to interpret the world around them, and how to feel about it. Being a parent means training your children in the way you want them to be . . . to be someone you can be proud of. Your children are an extension of you and a reflection of your parenting skills. If they don't do what you think they should with their lives and turn out the way you've imagined, then you will have failed, and everyone will know it. You believe children should honor their parents by living the life their parents have sacrificed to make for them. Anything less would be dishonorable. You pray every day that they won't launch off into this type of rebellion, because you honestly don't think you could accept or forgive that type of disrespectful behavior.

There may be some truth in that reaction. However, if you are giving unconditional love and acceptance, you realize that your children do not belong to you. You may have helped bring them into the world, but they're separate individuals born with a unique purpose that you quite possibly may never understand.

Love and acceptance, especially of your children, must by its very nature be given without conditions or restrictions. By design, each human is born with a unique personality and purpose. Of course, you want your children to have complete happiness, and you realize that being true to both of those unique aspects of personality and purpose is what will lead to complete fulfillment and happiness for your children. As much as you'd like to live their lives for them, give them the benefit of your experience, right all your wrongs through them, and protect them from hurt, pain, or disappointment, you cannot. In fact, the growth they'll experience from making their own mistakes is critical to realizing their potential. You can only love and accept them as they are . . . flawed . . . imperfect . . . trying . . . humans . . . sometimes failing, sometimes succeeding, always unique.

Parents teach their children up to a point at which the roles shift and the child becomes the teacher of the parent. If you're a parent who embraces that reality, loves your children unconditionally, and accepts those lessons, then you're practicing the principle of unconditional love and acceptance.

Scenario 3:

You've started volunteering with the Big Brothers organization. The "little brother" you have been matched with is a precious child, but he really has had it rough. His mother has four children by three different men. She was only married to one of them, but divorced him when he was sent to prison for armed robbery. She dropped out of high school to have the first baby and barely manages to make a meager living as a hotel maid. Both of her parents are drawing disability checks, and she aspires to do the same. Your "little brother," being the oldest of the children, is frequently placed in the position of caregiver to the younger three, which is ludicrous because he's barely mature enough to take care of himself. He's not getting much at home in the way of good examples and his head is all over the place. When he was playing on the basketball team at school, he thought he could get a scholarship, despite his slight five feet, five inch frame. Now that summer is here, he's decided he's going to be a professional skateboard rider.

✏ What would you think, feel, and do in this situation? Write your answer here.

_____

_____

_____

_____

_____

_____

_____

_____

_____

_____

_____

One could easily be inclined to think this boy is stuck in a cycle that will repeat itself. Some of it must be genetic. After all, look at his grandparents, drawing disability checks and making no attempt to better themselves. He'll never have the opportunities that someone born to a higher station would automatically have. He's just an average kid, nothing special as far as academics or athletics go. In fact, he may even be a below-average student. The lack of common sense or good judgment that led his mother to bear all those illegitimate children might have been passed on to him. And he spends more time with her, kidding himself about basketball scholarships and skateboarding competitions, than he spends with you. What can you do about his situation? The best you can do for him is to provide a break from a depressing environment, free from caring for his younger siblings, for a few pleasurable activities.

Now consider another possibility. It's true that these long-repeated patterns in families and neighborhoods are difficult to break. If, however, you're committed to being an inspiration to this child, you refuse to accept as permanent the limitations of his current situation. You realize that right now he can't begin to fathom the possibilities you see for him. But that just means you'll have to work harder to get through to him. You make it your mission to remove the blinders from his eyes and help him see beyond the boundaries of his life experience. You spend time thinking about his situation, trying to imagine what it feels like. You ask him questions about it and listen to his answers to discover his assumptions, his natural tendencies, and his interests and talents. You think about what you can say and do that would help invalidate his assumptions, open his mind, and expose him to new opportunities. You take him to do fun things, but always with a purpose in mind. And you're always teaching him . . . talking to him about life . . . sharing success stories to motivate him . . . helping him to discover resources within himself. If he suddenly wakes up and develops an interest in something that you know nothing about, you immediately become a student alongside him, supporting him in his exploration, all the while hoping to help him blossom as an individual. If this was your reaction to the scenario, then you're exhibiting the principle of being an inspiration.

Scenario 4:

Sometimes you just don't know how your mom and dad can really be your parents. Their way of life couldn't be more different than yours. They disapprove of everything you do. Nothing is ever good enough. And they're so narrow-minded. They can't even begin to consider that they might be wrong, and you might be right. They're both so judgmental and so critical and so smug about their opinions. You don't know how your sister and brother tolerate it. Sometimes you wonder if you were adopted.

☞ What would you think, feel, and do in this situation? Write your answer here.

_____

_____

_____

_____

_____

_____

_____

_____

_____

_____

_____

_____

_____

_____

_____

This situation can be so common in families, especially when parents exhibit the less than desirable response described in Scenario 2. While parents may be driven by a desire to be honored by their children, children naturally feel that it's important to be known, understood, and accepted, especially by their parents. One reaction to this scenario is based upon the importance of knowing that the people who brought you into the world approve of you, or at the very least don't disapprove of you. After all, if you can't make them love you, who can you make love you? If you could only make them understand why you've chosen this lifestyle. There's a perfectly good explanation, if they'd just shut up, stop arguing, and listen to you. You're so sick of fighting with them, but they're forcing you with their negative behavior to constantly defend yourself. And you're determined to win this debate. Nevertheless, it's getting to the point where you barely talk to them and never come to visit. It's all their fault. If they would just give you unconditional love and acceptance, none of this would be happening. As far as you're concerned, if they want a relationship with you, the ball is in their court.

Finger-pointing and blaming is an easy trap to fall into, especially in families where you're so entangled in one another's hearts and lives. And it's true parents should, hopefully, give unconditional love and acceptance to their children, although we all know there could be extreme cases in which this would actually be justifiably difficult. But most of the time the situation can be improved and possibly resolved by remembering one simple fact. Unconditional love and acceptance must flow in both directions. Your parents are not you, nor are you the same as your parents. Your parents, even though they may seem to have taken on many of the same characteristics, are also two unique individuals. The three of you are unique and different. Therefore, you'll never, by definition, see eye to eye on everything. You may never see eye to eye on anything at all. And that's okay. That's life. The fact is, whether one or both of your parents ever understands or approves of your life, or if they never do, that doesn't prevent you from being who you were born to be.

Just as you wouldn't ask a three-year-old child to decipher a calculus problem, don't ask your parents to decipher the mysteries of your life. They are who they are, just like every other person you meet is who they are—the product of genetics and life experiences—whether you understand or approve of them or not. Unconditional love and acceptance is something that must be given freely to all, if it's to work its magic, especially to those we don't understand, even if they are our parents.

If you responded to this scenario that unconditional love and acceptance must be given, even when it's not reciprocated . . . that you must love and accept the parents described in this scenario, even if you think they're wrong . . . that you should love the soul, if not the behavior, then you are exhibiting the principle of unconditional love and acceptance.

Scenario 5:

You've hired a young, hotshot fresh out of college. He had all the right education. His profile suggests he's a good talent match for the position. And he even had a little work experience gained through summer internships and co-op positions. He's confident and eager. You were glad to see it, because you had been shorthanded for a while and had become totally covered with more than you can handle. You were ready for someone to take some of the burden from you and gladly off-loaded some of your work to him.

Now that he's been here a few months, it's lightened the load in some ways. At least now you have someone to delegate to. But it hasn't been perfect. His experience and education really hadn't completely prepared him for the situations he would face here. And, in a few instances, he's probably messed things up more than he's helped. He's trying to use all those newfangled software programs and apply all these new methods with which you're not familiar. You thought you were hiring someone just like you, but realize now you didn't. You haven't said anything to him yet, but sometimes you wish you hadn't hired him. Maybe it would be easier to just go back to doing the work yourself.

✏ What would you think, feel, and do in this situation? Given your hectic situation, what's the scenario you think might play out over time? How do you honestly think you'd act toward this young employee? Write your answer here.

_____

_____

_____

_____

_____

_____

_____

_____

_____

_____

_____

_____

_____

Here's one possible reaction. The obvious fact is that a demanding, fast-paced business environment is difficult enough by itself, without the added dimension of dealing with maverick young kids, who don't know what they're doing, trying to make a name for themselves. The first thing you have to do, before this makes you a nervous wreck, is get this off your chest. That's what your colleagues are for. Around the coffeepot, in the conference room before the meeting starts, over drinks after work, you confide in them that this kid is driving you crazy. You tell story after story, recounting all the bonehead moves he's made. You have to laugh about it and relieve the stress to keep from lashing out at him. He's driving you crazy. You keep telling him what to do, but he's just not getting it. You can hardly stand to be around him. If he doesn't figure things out soon, you're going to have to figure out a way to pawn him off on somebody else in the company or just get rid of him. Sometimes it's just the wrong fit. And he's young. He can find another job.

Now look at it from a different perspective. It's true that, despite your best recruiting and hiring efforts, you sometimes end up with the wrong fit. But you shouldn't jump to that conclusion, especially not if you're practicing the behavior of being a good coach and learner.

Even if you didn't establish a coaching system to support this young man when he first came to work, it's never too late to start. The first step in establishing that system is to provide clear expectations and examples of what it looks like to be successful in the role. As his manager, what do you want and need from this employee? What does he need from you to be enabled? What do you or others need to teach him? How can you model this desired behavior and performance level for him so that he has tangible understanding of what you need? How can you provide regular feedback, especially in the beginning, to help him gauge his progress, to reinforce what he's doing well, and to provide additional guidance in areas where he still has some development work to do?

If you're practicing these coaching behaviors, one important element is that you maintain his trust in you as his coach. So, while you may sometimes be frustrated, you don't undermine his reputation with others in the company. Besides, the regular, constructive discussions you're having go a long way to neutralize your frustration and typically correct his inappropriate behavior before it rises to the nuisance level. In fact, you're even learning from him.

As he becomes more and more familiar with what you want him to accomplish, he's showing you how the work can be streamlined using his computer skills. You've also discussed some new methods. Sometimes he's a little overzealous, and you have to convince him that his ideas are overkill. But there have been occasions when he taught you something new that really enhanced your overall results.

Being a coach means being a teacher, role model, and learner. The two-way street of communication and sharing always benefits both parties . . . even if the employee is the wrong fit for the position. If you responded to this scenario in this manner, then you realize this and are exhibiting the principle of being a good coach and lifelong learner.

Scenario 6:

You know Joan through your friend Linda. Linda was your college roommate, so you two have a lot of history linking you to one another. But you just met Joan a few months ago through Linda, and you really don't know much about her. Now that you all have kids in the same school, you see Joan more and more. You, Linda, Joan, and all the mothers have your hands full with work, home, husband, and kids. You're always either on the run or have a million things on your mind. You often feel like you're juggling more than anyone should have to handle.

✏ What would you think, feel, and do in this situation? Given your hectic situation, what is the scenario that you think might play out over time? How do you honestly think you would act toward your new acquaintance Joan? Write your answer here.

_____

_____

_____

_____

_____

_____

_____

_____

_____

_____

_____

_____

_____

_____

_____

_____

Here's one likely alternative. When Joan is around you and Linda, she seems very nice. She laughs at your stories, and your husband's unreasonable demands, and your kids' latest hijinks. She's very soft-spoken and even-tempered with her kids. Most of the time, you and Linda are chatting away so much about your kids and how the two of you never imagined in school that you would end up at your kids' PTA together, that you hardly even notice Joan is there. She's a good listener. It makes you feel better just to have someone laugh with you about your crazy life.

That's a highly likely scenario. Now consider this. Linda answers the phone one day to find you on the other end of the line almost breathless with excitement. "Linda, why didn't you tell me that Joan is a writer?" you practically scream into the phone. "You know I've wanted to write ever since we were in college and here, right under our noses, is someone who is actually doing it! I'm so impressed!"

Linda replies, "I never knew! I just met Joan when I volunteered at little Timmy's class. We helped with a couple birthday parties. I thought about asking her over afterwards for coffee, but I had such a mess at home."

"Well, she's the most down-to-earth person you could ever meet, Linda," you explain to your old college friend. "I can't imagine she'd care about a few dirty dishes. And can you guess what kind of books she writes? They're all about family psychology! She even practiced as a family counselor before her children were born. I've already learned so much from her. I rushed right out to buy one of her books. Linda, it feels like it was written just for me. I can't wait to talk to my husband about some of her recommendations."

"Wow," Linda replies, stunned.

"And do you know she lost her husband last year? It's so hard for her to find time to write, now that she doesn't have any help with the kids. So I've volunteered to pick up her kids with mine two days a week and bring them here for dinner with us. They get along great together, and what are two more mouths to feed? It's no trouble at all for me, and it'll give her time to do her work. Lord knows we all need more of her books!"

In this second scenario, what we see is the result of our main character making a connection with Joan, whom she has met through her old friend Linda. It's easy, with the hectic nature of family life today, to get so inwardly focused and wrapped up in our own lives that it simply requires too much effort to connect with someone else. It's difficult enough to stay connected with old friends, not to mention establish a connection with a new acquaintance. But what this story demonstrates is that even in the midst of our very full lives, there can always be something found in another person that's interesting, exciting, energizing, and even beneficial to us.

Many people believe that others come into our lives for a reason. Perhaps Joan is in the other mothers' lives in this scenario because they can learn something they really need to know in order to improve their situation. And the other mothers are in Joan's life because they can provide the appreciation, stability, and support she really needs at this time in her life. Discovering mutual purpose begins with making a connection with someone, versus settling for a casual hello in the drop-off and pick-up line at school every day. The principle of making a connection requires an outward focus on others, a curiosity, and it requires effort. But the rewards far outweigh the effort.

Scenario 7:

Going back to school as an adult certainly hasn't been any easier. If anything, it's been more difficult than when you were in college the first time . . . many years ago. Now you actually care what grade you make. How can you ever look your kids in the eye again and demand As if you don't even make them yourself? Plus, you have the added pressure of the tuition reimbursement program at work. True, you don't have to make As to qualify for the reimbursement. But you do have to turn in your grade reports. Now not only will everyone in the Human Resources department know your grades, but also your manager who thankfully didn't look at a transcript when he hired you. How embarrassing it would be to hold a leadership role in the company and turn in anything less than straight As!

The overachiever mentality that drove you to go back to school at this age in the first place is officially kicked into overdrive. Complicating this situation is the crazy group approach that's used in this program. It's hard enough to make As doing your own work. Now you have to drag four other people along with you like boat anchors. No way are you going to let them jeopardize your A! And, to make matters worse, they get to rate your team participation at the end of each course, and it has an impact on your grade! The grades you make in this Master's program will probably have a big bearing on whether you can get accepted into a Doctoral program somewhere. This is too important to be left to chance.

✎ What would you think, feel, and do in this situation? Given the pressure you've placed on yourself, what's the scenario that you think might play out over time? How do you honestly think you would act toward your group members? Write your answer here.

_____

_____

_____

_____

_____

_____

_____

_____

_____

_____

_____

_____

_____

_____

Here's one likely reaction to this scenario. You meet in study group every week to work on your group assignments, and you're trying to work together. But sometimes you think maybe you should have enrolled in a Master's program that's structured differently. You don't even know these people. They may be only marginal "C" students at best. This isn't a popularity contest. It doesn't matter if they like you or not. You have to look out for number one. The only person's work you can trust is your own.

You suffer through the group projects because you have to let each group member contribute. But you try repeatedly to tell them how to do their part, or at least insist they let you critique and edit their work. You have to work twice as hard to maintain control of this situation. Sometimes it feels like you're doing all the work. In fact, they're delegating a lot more to you and leaving more and more of it for you to do. "If we do it, you'll just change it anyway," they say. Well, okay, if you have to do most of the work, so be it. All you have to do at the end is to fool them into giving you a decent rating. Besides, their rating is only a small percentage of your grade, and when this program is over, you'll never see these people again anyway.

Now here's another possible conclusion to this scenario. You realize that while this is a new and uncomfortable situation for you, it's part of the learning experience. After all, no one exists in a vacuum. It's unlikely you'll have the opportunity to practice these learned concepts without interference from others after you graduate from the program. You won't. So you seize this opportunity to practice applying these concepts with others through the program's group projects before you actually have to go out in the real world and do it. And, because you're focused on the principle of believing in others, you actively work to overcome the doubts, distrust, and misunderstandings that result naturally from your apprehension about returning to school.

First, you talk openly with your teammates about your concerns. You share with them how important it is to you to make an A in this course. You listen and share with one another your goals, desires, strengths, and weaknesses. As a result of this honest and frank dialogue, you discover that every member of the group has his or her own similar concerns. You learn what each can contribute and you gain the confidence you need to trust your teammates. It's not that you learned you could believe in them. If you hadn't believed in them in the first place, you never would have shared your innermost thoughts and motivations with them.

Practicing a belief in others means this is always your default position, even before you have visible evidence that it's well-founded. After all, it's not their past performance you're believing in, it's their inner, perhaps even undiscovered, potential. No, engaging in open dialogue is not the means to gain belief. It's the means to turn off your dinosaur left brain that's always seeking to protect you, even from imagined threats. And, lo and behold, what do you discover in the very first group project? Your teammate Julie is much more creative than you ever could have been. Your first project is a rousing success . . .

and it was all her idea. If you imagined the scenario playing out in this manner, then you're exhibiting the behaviors that characterize a belief in others.

Exercise 2

Now that you've had the previous scenarios to consider, you should begin to recognize the situations in your own life in which you're teaching others. The purpose of this next exercise is to reflect on some of those situations, as well as the lessons you're teaching.

Here are the directions for the exercise.

1. Think about the four areas discussed at the beginning of this chapter: **family, work, social,** and **self**. Think of at least **one example from each of these four areas** in your own life.

2. Using the following templates, answer the questions for each of your four examples. If you can think of more than one example, use additional sheets of paper.

3. Work through as many examples needed to gain a clear picture of how you're teaching those around you.

4. Be honest and challenge yourself.

Optional:

5. You can keep your reflections totally confidential, or you may find that you benefit from hearing yourself discuss this aloud with a trusted friend or family member.

6. If you choose to do the exercise with a partner, ask him or her to read the question aloud, then to listen to your response without comment or judgment. You can describe a situation that's unfolding now or one from your past. Have them jot down their own thoughts as they listen to your answer.

7. Afterwards, if you want feedback, ask them to share their thoughts with you. If you don't ask for feedback, then they can keep their notes and use them for their own reflection and growth.

Introduction

☞ Whom are you trying, or whom have you tried, to teach?

_____

_____

☞ Briefly describe the situation.

_____

_____

Unconditional Love & Acceptance

☞ What unique qualities did you see in the person?

_____

_____

☞ How did you affirm, build up, or encourage this person?

_____

_____

☞ What did you accept in this person that you didn't like or understand?

_____

_____

✏ What did you see about this person's past that has led them to where they are now?

_____

_____

✏ What did you find that you share in common with this individual?

_____

_____

Commitment to a Vision

✏ What thoughts, feelings, hunches, or dreams did you have regarding the possibilities in this situation? How did you act upon them?

_____

_____

✏ What barriers did you identify that are inhibiting this person's progress toward the possibilities? What did you do to help remove them?

_____

_____

✏ What extra effort did you put forth to help this person learn and grow?

_____

_____

✏ In what way did you temporarily subordinate your own interests to teach and help this person advance toward the person they were born to be?

_____

_____

Structure & Organization

✏ How did you address the person's need for safety, security, and respect in this situation?

_____

_____

✏ How did you establish trust with the other person?

_____

_____

✏ How did you facilitate the other person's growth as an individual?

_____

_____

Be Inspiring

✏ How did this situation present an opportunity for you to help this other person to move closer to his or her one true self?

_____

_____

✏ What paradigms did you find to be limiting the other person's self-actualization?

_____

_____

✏ How did you help the other person explore their current paradigms?

_____

_____

✏ What inspiration did you give to the other person?

_____

_____

Make a Connection

✏ Why were you in this person's life at this particular time?

_____

_____

✏ What was the **other person's** most important need in the situation?

_____

_____

☞ What was **your** most important need in the situation?

_____

_____

☞ Did you judge or categorize the person based upon initial interactions, or did you seek to understand how they perceive the situation? Did you make a connection with this person? What could you do?

_____

_____

☞ How did you interact with the other person?

_____

_____

☞ What were you trying to teach?

_____

_____

☞ Why were you trying to teach that lesson? What was your motivation?

_____

_____

☞ What were you trying to accomplish? What results were you trying to bring about?

_____

_____

Believe in Others

☞ Did you remove the words "don't" and "can't" from your interaction with this person?

_____

_____

☞ How did you demonstrate respect for the unique journey the person is on?

_____

_____

☞ How did you show this person your belief in them and their potential?

_____

_____

☞ Did you try to control the other person and/or the situation? What did you do? What assumptions, fears, or needs drove your behavior? How can you avoid doing this in the future?

_____

_____

_____

✏ Did you exhibit negativity in your attitude, comments, body language, or approach toward the person and the situation? What did you do? How can you avoid doing this in the future?

_____

_____

_____

_____

Be a Coach & Lifelong Learner

✏ Did you look for the lessons you can learn in the situation? What are they?

_____

_____

✏ Were you more focused on what you could give this person or on what you could get from this person?

_____

_____

✏ How did this situation present an opportunity for you to move closer to your one true self?

_____

_____

☛ How did you model your teaching for this person, i.e., turn your words into action?

_____

_____

☛ How did you create an environment where mistakes are tolerated?

_____

_____

☛ How did you give positive reinforcement?

_____

_____

Summary

☛ Which of the seven principles did you perform well in this situation?

_____

_____

☛ Which of the seven principles could you perform better with this person?

_____

_____

✏ Overall, what are your feelings about the situation?

_____

_____

✏ How would you *like* to feel about the situation?

_____

_____

✏ Did you unconsciously project your own fears, needs, or desires onto the other person? Which ones?

_____

_____

✏ Did you limit the possible choices and options in the situation? If so, how?

_____

_____

✏ Can you think of five better, more mutually beneficial options for the situation?

_____

_____

☞ If the situation being analyzed is still occurring, what is the worst possible outcome you can imagine for the other person? For you?

_____

_____

☞ What is the best possible outcome you can imagine for the other person? For you?

_____

_____

☞ What is an action you would be willing to do yourself, right now, to help make that best possible outcome more probable for you and the other person?

_____

_____

☞ If the situation being analyzed occurred in the past, what was the result of the situation for the other person?

_____

_____

☞ What was the result for you?

_____

_____

✏ Overall, what did you do well?

_____

_____

✏ What could you have done differently? What will you do differently next time?

_____

_____

We sometimes think or hear ourselves comment, "I don't know why I think/feel/act that way. I just do." That's because each of us is influenced by that which we carry in our shadow and unconscious mind. Although it is unconscious and seldom explored, every day it is influencing how we act and react in situations like those we just explored in the previous exercise.

This next exercise is designed to scratch the surface of the unconscious mind and begin to shed light on that which lies beneath the teacher you already are. The word association method is a psychological test typically found as one part of a comprehensive test battery. Here it is used simply as a tool to encourage introspection into areas of your thoughts and feelings on which you may not have previously reflected.

Exercise 3

Word association is intended to reveal associative connections between stimulus words (i.e., the provided word) and free verbal responses (i.e., your response word). The purpose of this exercise is to expose some of your deeply engrained tendencies to make you more aware of your current teaching style and how you may be perceived by those you're teaching in your circle of influence. Here are the directions for the exercise.

1. You're asked to supply predicate responses, meaning your response word should express judgment about the provided word. For

example, if the provided word was "marriage" and you responded "forever," your word would express your personal judgment about the institution of marriage.

2. You should respond to each provided word as quickly as possible. Don't dwell on each word. Your first, immediate reaction to the provided word will be the most reflective of how you are likely to feel in everyday situations.

3. THERE IS NO RIGHT OR WRONG ANSWER. Be honest. Write down what first pops into your mind, even if it surprises you.

4. If you find that you have to pause longer than usual on a particular word, place an asterisk (*) beside the provided word. We'll reflect on your responses after you conclude the exercise.

Learning	_____	Past	_____
Growth	_____	Future	_____
Problem	_____	Freedom	_____
Belief	_____	Failure	_____
Possibility	_____	Discipline	_____
Fear	_____	Individuality	_____
Trust	_____	Love	_____
Challenge	_____	Spirituality	_____
Security	_____	Self	_____
Dreams	_____	Society	_____
Opportunity	_____	History	_____
Progress	_____	Boundaries	_____
Children	_____	Happiness	_____
Men	_____	Present	_____
Fate	_____	Work	_____
Genetics	_____	Success	_____
Wealth	_____	Heredity	_____
Selflessness	_____	Destiny	_____
Identity	_____	Power	_____
Sacrifice	_____	Connectedness	_____
Service	_____	Fame	_____
Team	_____	Religion	_____
Women	_____	Helping	_____
Mistakes	_____	Abundance	_____

Copy the provided word into one of the three boxes below, based upon your judgment of the word. For example, if your response to the provided word "work" was "drudgery," that is a negative judgment, so write the word "work" in the "negative" box below. If your answer, instead, was "fun," which is a positive judgment, write the word "work" in the "positive" box. If your response was something more "neutral," such as "daily," write the word "work" in the "neutral" column.

NEGATIVE	NEUTRAL	POSITIVE

Next, for every word on which you paused or hesitated to determine your response (i.e., the words marked with an asterisk) copy those words into the box below.

Now let's analyze your results. Were you surprised by your response to any of the words? Did any stimulate an especially negative reaction? Using a highlighter, mark the words for which your judgment surprised you or was especially negative. Spend a few minutes thinking about why you reacted in this manner.

How about the words on which you hesitated? Why do you think you paused? It's possible you were surprised to see the word in the list and simply was caught off guard. However, clinicians would say a delayed response indicates an issue with the word, although this will not be true in every case. Spend a few minutes reflecting on the words on which you hesitated. What comes to mind when you look at the words? How is this thought or feeling affecting your attitude toward the words and the situations they represent?

DELAYED-RESPONSE WORDS

For analysis purposes, copy the words on which your response was "negative," "neutral," or "delayed" into the following box.

"I feel less than positive or possibly have issues with . . ."

This exercise has been designed to help you verbalize your deep thoughts and feelings. Verbalizations are a useful tool for building self-awareness because they reflect ideation, the forming of ideas. We form ideas based upon that which we initially interpret through our senses of sight, smell, touch, taste, and hearing. The resulting idea, which we verbalized with this exercise, can be an indication of how we would respond to the stimuli presented during an interaction with others. If we're uncertain about our thoughts and feelings regarding a certain situation, or if we're negative or ambivalent, in the spur of the moment we'll act out of that uncertainty, ambivalence, or negative posture. Whether we're aware of it or not, it will be perceptible to the other person engaged in the interaction with us.

So let's explore some of the possible responses to the word association. (Remember: there are no right or wrong answers. We're just looking for insights into the teacher you already are and the lessons you're teaching those in your circle of influence.)

For the word "possibility" two possible responses are "limited" or "limitless." If we believe there is a limit to what can be achieved, this will certainly be perceived by those around us. Moreover, a deep-seated belief of this nature, or even uncertainty or neutrality on the subject, would hamper our ability to be inspiring to those around us. The principles of being an inspiration, believing in others, and even being a good coach and lifelong learner, require a feeling of limitless possibilities.

The word "fear" is an interesting one because it's so closely related to the normal functioning of our left brain. In the word association, we might use predicates like "important," "warning," "real," or "rational." Any response such as these would recognize the fact that fear is a natural protection mechanism that originates in the left brain, which is always seeking to keep us safe. But we need to remember this protection mechanism often works overtime. It convinces us we shouldn't try something new or different, because it might result in failure. (Or, is it fear of success?)

If we recognized this nature of fear, then we might have instead used words like "imagined," "irrational," or "something to be overcome" to describe "fear" in our word association. Recognizing that fear often originates from our outdated paradigms, limiting mental models, and overactive protection mechanism, we must see fear in most cases as something to be overcome if we are to truly exhibit the seven principles of effective teaching. In all seven areas, and especially believing in others and staying committed to a vision, we can't allow ourselves to hesitate or be ruled by fear. If we do, then our "possibilities" truly will be "limited."

Similar to the word "possibility," we have the words "challenge" and "dreams." It's possible that we would equate a "challenge" with a "problem." If we're challenged, that means we have a problem, right? As far as "dreams" go, if we're adults and still dreaming, we're dwelling on something "foolish," "unrealistic," and probably "unachievable," correct? On the other hand, we could have responded to the word "challenge" with "opportunity" and to the word "dreams" with the word "achievable" or "guides." We need not view challenges and dreams in a negative sense. In fact, because challenges and dreams present us with the opportunity and motivation to learn and grow, we must cultivate a positive impression of these situations if we are to successfully practice the seven principles of effective teaching.

Let's look at two more, "learning" and "growth." Quick, think of the answer to this question. "When did you finish your education?"

Some of you would most likely respond with the year you completed your last grade in school or the age at which you graduated from high school or college. That response is aligned with a paradigm that "learning" and "growth" are "temporary," occurring "in school." If, however, we truly believe that "learning" is "lifelong" and personal "growth" is "continuous," we'll be more able to freely practice the seven principles, which will make us far more effective teachers to all those around us.

We can further analyze the lesson of the word associations by comparing them to the preceding scenario exercise. Do you see patterns in the word association that manifested themselves in your reaction to the scenarios?

Let's consider scenario number seven in which you're going back to school in a program where a group structure predominates. A negative reaction to that scenario may have been influenced by a negative or uncertain feeling about several of the words in the word association exercise, such as problem, belief, men, possibility, fear, women, trust, selflessness, team, connectedness, or helping. Likewise, a complementary and overly positive emphasis on words like security, freedom, individuality, self, success, and power would almost certainly make it very difficult to function effectively in the group situation presented in scenario number seven.

We see from this analysis how a negative feeling toward some ideas and emotions and a positive feeling toward others combine to produce a certain response in a given situation. It's not just the ideas or situations toward which you had a negative reaction that may hinder you in delivering the seven principles. It's the unique combination of the negatives and the positives. How are your negative, neutral, and positive attitudes combining to make you the kind of teacher you are? How do you think the result is perceived by those in your circle of influence?

To continue your reflection on the teacher you already are and the messages you're sending, look back over your responses to the scenarios at the beginning of this chapter. Compare your reaction to the scenarios to your responses to the word associations. In what ways do you see a connection between your responses to the two exercises? Do you see patterns or inconsistencies? Did you provide responses that reflect how you really are or how you would like to be? Can you think of real-life situations you've experienced similar to those presented in the scenarios? How did you react in your real-life example? What patterns do you see in your personal examples? What ideas seem to drive your behavior most? Do you need to find a better balance in order to practice the seven principles more routinely? On which areas do you need to focus now in order to achieve that balance?

Exercise 4

The previous exercises were designed to hold a mirror up in front of you so you could see the teacher those around you see. This exercise is designed to begin excavating deeper inside, beneath the surface that's seen by others, to the strengths possessed deep within—strengths that you may not be utilizing fully. Here are the directions for this exercise.

1. Begin by making a list of all your positive attributes. Think about everything you've read in this book up to this point. What did you read about with which you easily identified? When did you find yourself thinking, "I'm good at that," or "That's what I do"? List everything about yourself that you know to be a strength.

2. Remember, the most important thing about these exercises is to be honest with yourself. No one but you will ever see your responses. This exercise is for you. Don't be shy or modest when listing your responses. Just be realistic with yourself. Don't list those you simply admire or to which you aspire. List the attributes that you know you possess.

My Personal Attributes (use an additional piece of paper if necessary):

Now, using the legend below, beside each of your personal attributes write the number of the principle to which it is related.

1. Be Committed to a Vision

2. Give Unconditional Love and Acceptance

3. Make a Connection

4. Be Inspiring

5. Be Structured and Organized

6. Be a Coach and Lifelong Learner

7. Believe in Others

For instance, if you wrote that one attribute you possess is a "true belief in the unlimited potential of others," place the number "7" beside that attribute.

Example:
Truly believe in unlimited potential of others (7)

> NOTE: It is possible for one of your attributes to be related to more than one of the seven principles.

Example:
Enjoy creating a structure in which others are
motivated to learn and grow. (4) (5)

After completing this mapping of your attributes to the seven principles, notice how many of the principles you're already demonstrating. Which ones are you demonstrating most? These are your strengths. Are there any principles that you're barely exhibiting or not at all? These may be your weaknesses that need to be managed. Let's talk about strengths and weaknesses.

Donald Clifton and Paula Nelson, in their book *Soar With Your Strengths*, claim that there's a national obsession with "fixing what's wrong." If we're not good at something, we must put forth more effort to become good at it. We have to focus on those weaknesses in order to fix them and improve ourselves. That's the American way.

Not true, says Clifton and Nelson. One example they cite is writing a term paper. Focusing on eliminating all the spelling and syntax errors doesn't guarantee a paper worthy of an A. You'll have created an error-free paper, but not necessarily an excellent one. Great writing, just like any other form of personal greatness, is about transferring the strength of an individual's great thoughts to paper. Excellence, they posit, is not achieved through the elimination of weaknesses, but only by focusing on strengths while managing weaknesses.

They also point out that this assertion seems counterintuitive in a culture where our media is rife with stories of all the disastrous downfalls of individuals and organizations. But studying why some businesses or individuals fail will not teach us why others are successful. Similarly, studying our weaknesses will not teach us how to be stronger. This fact debunks the myth that if you really want to improve, you shouldn't invest time in what you're already good at but instead work on your weak areas in order to develop to your fullest. Again, not true, says Clifton and Nelson. You only need awareness of your weaknesses so you can manage or compensate for them with your strengths. To truly improve you must invest your greatest energy in the area where you have the greatest potential for a payback on that investment . . . your strengths.

The misguided theory of fixing weaknesses is based on a mindset that would purport that we're all clones with the same kind of strengths and potential. We know this to be false, even though we still fall victim to these "power of positive thinking" theories, which seek to convince us we can do it all if we just try harder. Have you ever heard a teacher say, "He's so good at English grammar. He just needs to focus on improving his math skills." Or how about this? Have you ever heard a basketball coach say about one of his players, "He's such a natural shooter and a very intelligent player. He just needs to improve his speed and quickness."

I was a basketball player in my youth. I still remember the first time I held a ball in my hands and lofted it goalward. I remember how the dimpled cover felt in my hands, how the seams rolled off my fingers, how natural it felt. Sometimes, I couldn't believe the shots I hit. Yet I had absolute confidence. I thought every shot was going in, and a large percentage of them did. This was my game. I understood it. I knew where everyone was on the floor, and where they were most likely to go. I understood the strategy of the game and loved trying to outthink opponents for the win. This was especially enjoyable against the more physically endowed teams, because I wasn't blessed with that same speed and agility.

Those were my weaknesses. But I and the astute coaches I had throughout my career recognized that we gained nothing by focusing on my weaknesses. They were what they were. I was only able to work on those areas and improve to a point. So my coaches avoided creating situations that would expose my weaknesses, and I limited the amount of time invested in those weaknesses and instead invested time in improving my strengths. I spent hours on my court at home and in the gym at school with my dad or my coach rebounding and throwing the ball back to me, over and over and over again, perfecting my technique and rhythm, until it was automatic from anywhere. My way to excel on the court was to be in a position to shoot each time the ball touched my hands, while not allowing my lack of quickness to hamper me or the team. If the person I was guarding was quicker than I and occasionally got around me to score, then I had to be sure to score twice as much as she did. I excelled with my strengths and managed my weaknesses.

According to Clifton and Nelson, in the simplest terms, you manage weaknesses by finding out what you don't do well, and you stop doing it. Here's another real example of that. For the past six years, I worked for Ken. During that time, we developed a working relationship that enabled both of us to soar with our strengths. When we had a party to recognize Ken's accomplishments, he summed it up this way.

He said, "I always wanted to be a leader who understood his people and was a sensitive, caring, people-person kind of manager. I knew I wanted to be that kind of leader, but I had no idea how to do it. I was good at financial stuff. I understood all the business elements. But I didn't know people. You, my staff, did that for me, especially the female members of my staff. You taught me how to care about my employees and build a family at work. You made me the kind of leader I wanted to be."

As I listened to Ken's remarks, I looked around the room at the faces there. Ken had always had more women on his staff than any of the other senior executives. At times, it had even been the source of a few good-natured jokes. But now, as I looked not only at the women in the room but also at the men, I recognized the secret to Ken's greatness. Ken had surrounded himself not with people like himself but with people who complemented him . . . people whose strengths compensated for his weaknesses. And then he listened and allowed each one to do what they did best.

I reflected on many of the conversations Ken and I had over my years of working for him. He always made me feel important and valuable to his team, because he knew he needed what I had to offer. His behavior enabled me to soar with my strengths. And I had seen him grow too. He had improved some of his weaknesses during that time. But no doubt about it, Ken had excelled because he soared with his strengths and managed his weaknesses by building a staff that was strong where he knew he was weak.

That's the lesson about weaknesses. Don't ignore them, because they'll hinder you if you do. Work on them because you can improve to some degree. But don't invest all your time in your weaknesses. Just be sure you're aware of them and that you manage them. The lesson about managing weaknesses is summed up in the familiar *Serenity Prayer*:

God, grant me the power to accept the things I cannot change, the courage to change the things I can, and the wisdom to know the difference.

What does this mean with regard to exhibiting the seven principles of effective teaching? Does this mean that if we're weak in a particular principle that we can just stop doing it? Absolutely not. All seven principles are crucial to being the best kind of teacher who can enable and empower others to fulfill their potential. What it does mean is that we need to be aware of the principles in which we are weak, improve as much as we possibly can, get creative about compensating for those weaknesses, and above all excel with our strengths.

Now let's explore your all-important strengths. Clifton and Nelson propose that we find out what we do well, and do more of it! These are your strengths, and that's where you should invest the majority of your self-improvement efforts.

When the coach of the 1984 Chinese Olympic gold medal-winning Ping-Pong team was asked about his philosophy, he replied, "If you develop your strengths to the maximum, the strength becomes so great, it overwhelms the weaknesses." The long-standing gold medal success of the Chinese Ping-Pong team provided clear evidence of the validity of his philosophy.

Clifton and Nelson define a strength as a pattern of behavior, thoughts, and feelings that produces a high degree of satisfaction and pride, generates both psychic and/or financial rewards, and presents measurable progress toward excellence. By focusing on the key words of behavior, thoughts, and feelings in their definition, they broaden it beyond the usual emphasis on physical strengths and behaviors to encompass motives and drives. Strengths and attributes are more than just the obvious.

One of my strengths in basketball was not just my obvious shooting ability, but also my determination to put forth more effort than those who were more physically endowed than I. Ken's strength wasn't just his financial and operational business prowess, but also his self-awareness and astuteness at building and inspiring a team whose joint capability exceeded the ability of any one single member of the team. You're probably not giving yourself credit for all your strengths.

Go back to the exercise where you listed your personal attributes. Revisit the list you created for yourself. What can you think of now to add to your list? What other strengths do you have?

After you've completed adding new strengths to your list, move on to this step. How can you focus on soaring with your strengths, while managing your weaknesses? Brainstorm some ideas here:

✍ Ways I can leverage and apply my strengths to teach and facilitate others' learning and growth:

_____

_____

_____

_____

_____

_____

_____

_____

_____

_____

_____

_____

✐ Weaknesses and the ways I can manage my weaknesses:

_____

_____

_____

_____

_____

_____

_____

_____

_____

_____

_____

_____

_____

_____

_____

_____

For more of Clifton and Nelson's practical ideas and suggestions, read *Soar With Your Strengths*, published by Dell Publishing in 1992. Good additional reading is *Now Discover Your Strengths*, coauthored by Clifton with Marcus Buckingham of the Gallup Organization, published by The Free Press in 2001.

The Teacher You Could Be

Deep inside man dwell these slumbering powers:
powers that would astonish him, that he never
dreamed of possessing; forces that would revolutionize
his life if aroused and put into action.

– Orison Swett Marden,
Editor, *Success Magazine*, 1848-1924

Six

You're still reading! Good for you! In the previous chapter, we dug deep to explore the teacher you already are. This is thoughtful work, and making it this far is a major step forward. Hang in here with me. The payoff on this investment is huge! Now that we've examined the teacher you are, we need to spend some time digging deeper to discover the teacher you could be.

The good news of lifelong development is that we possess virtually limitless potential. We're on the journey, always *becoming* what we could be. We're all driven. Even if we reach that pinnacle of self-actualization described by Maslow, we can always be expanding, enhancing, and improving the definition of self. Why is that true? It's true because we're students, constantly exposed to opportunities to learn and grow from and through others. That's where I want to begin our first exercise.

Exercise 1:

The purpose of this exercise is to start you on a path of being a good student—a path on which you notice the lessons in your everyday interactions with others. Here are the directions for this exercise.

1. In the following template, make a list in the left-hand column of all the people with whom you enjoy spending time. These are the people in your life now you like to be around.

2. In the second column, write the reason you like to be around this person. What is it about them that makes the time you spend together enjoyable.

3. Finish those two columns, then proceed directly to the next exercise.

4. Leave the third column blank for now.

People with whom I enjoy spending time:	Why?	Affirmations

After completing the first two columns above, continue on to the next exercise. Here are the directions for that exercise.

1. In the following template, in the first column, make a list of all the people who have made a positive impression or positive impact on you from birth to the present. These will be people who stand out in your memory in a good way. They could be family members, neighbors, authority figures, friends, or acquaintances.

2. Because we're looking at the period of time from birth to the present, you should have some new names that didn't appear on the list you made in the previous template. Write those additional names here in column one.

3. In column two, write what this person did, how they did it, and/or why they had a positive impact on you.

4. For now, leave the third column blank.

People who have had a positive impact on me:	Why?	Affirmations

When you're finished, look at your two lists. Reflect on how the people from your past made you feel, as well as how those who are still in your life make you feel now. Notice how warm and peaceful it makes you feel to think about these people. What is it about these people that enables them to have this impact on you? What do you believe are their strengths? What do they do best? How does that have such a positive impact on you?

Look at your two lists and ask yourself these questions. Which of the seven principles do you see reflected in each person's actions toward you? Which people made a unique connection with you and made you feel important as an individual? Which ones believed in you, even if you didn't believe in yourself? Who inspired you? Who gave you unconditional love and made you feel accepted . . . just the way you are? Who gave you the structure within which you could excel? Who was a good coach and role model for you? Who showed you a vision of the possibilities? Reflect on these questions, and notice how frequently the seven principles were present in the behavior of these people who made such a positive and lasting impression.

Now go back to the first list and fill in the third column, following these directions.

1. Read what you wrote in the second column. Think about why you enjoy being around this person.

2. In the third column, turn this into an affirmation, beginning with the words, "I will . . . " For example, if I wrote that I like to spend time with Mary Ann "because she is so positive and upbeat about everyone and everything," then in column three I would write, "I will maintain a positive attitude at all times."

3. Do this same thing in column three of the second template too. If, for example, in the second template I wrote that Mrs. Isbill had a positive impact on me "because she inspired me to grow beyond my perceived limitations and be all that I could be," then in column three of the second template I would write, "I will find a way to be an inspiration to others, especially those who feel their possibilities are limited and who most need inspiration."

4. When you've finished the third column, reflect on the two completed templates. Consider the ways you're already exhibiting

these behaviors. Think about the situations in which you have the opportunity to practice those you aren't regularly exhibiting.

Now that you have your set of affirmations, it's time to begin keeping your journal. Here, I'm going to give you the same recommendation that Tom Bird gives his students. Purchase a journal with unlined pages, if possible. The blank sheets of paper will prevent your left brain from immediately beginning to place boundaries on your thinking. It will allow you to be as free and creative as your right brain can be.

Copy into your journal the contents of the previous exercise in this chapter: the list of all the people you like to spend time with, the list of people who have made a positive impression or had a positive impact on your life, why that's true, and the "I will" affirmation statements you produced.

You may want to spend some time, as I have in this book, writing in your journal about those people who had a positive impact on you. Write the memories you have of this person. Capture the stories that are most prominent in your memory. Write about how they helped make your life better.

You may even want to send some of your stories to them. Many people never have the chance to know the lasting impact they have on others. Receiving that confirmation and positive reinforcement can be very beneficial to their learning and growth. It will not only make them feel good, it reverses the roles of teacher and student momentarily and allows them to be your student as you teach them what they're doing well and what to do more of.

After you've started your journal, you can begin tracking your progress against your "I will" affirmation statements. On a daily or weekly basis, reflect on how well you did at living out those commitments. When and with whom did you do it? What did you do? Which of the seven principles were you exercising most? How did it feel? What did you learn? Do you need to do anything differently next time? Reflect on the day or week that just passed. Did you miss any opportunities to act on your commitments to yourself? Did you fail to exhibit the seven principles? How will you make sure you do the right thing next time? If you're able to see immediate results of your actions, for instance if the person does something they didn't think they could do because of your encouragement, or if they tell you directly that you've made a positive impact on them, be sure to capture that in your journal. Write what they did or said, how it made you feel, and record in your journal entries your renewed commitment to exhibit more of those behaviors.

You may be struggling with the previous assignment, but I doubt it. I feel certain that you were able to produce names of people you like to be around, as well as people who have made a positive impression on you. But I had one instance, when I first started writing this book, that startled me. Upon telling my best friend that the book was about my great teachers, I noticed a concerned, faraway look on her face. When I asked what was wrong, she replied, "I never had any teachers like that." While it bothered and worried me for a time, I now believe she simply had the wrong perspective on what a teacher is and who our great teachers really are. I can't imagine that anyone could have read the initial chapters of this book and not thought of some names to put on their lists.

Nevertheless, I do recognize that as we all have had *good* teachers in our lives, by the same token there are also *bad* ones. These are the people who send negative signals. They exhibit the opposite of the seven principles. Erikson would say they're stuck in one of the eight stages of psychosocial development, unable or unwilling to resolve the conflicts that trap them there. Maslow would say they've failed to satisfy the lesser needs that would enable them to be self-actualized. Jung would say they haven't dealt with the issues lurking in their unconscious mind. All these theories would be correct.

There are two important points here for us to remember. First, these people are still students, and we have the opportunity to be their teacher by exhibiting the seven principles in our behavior toward them. Second, they can still be our teacher too. Armed with our new sense of awareness about these matters, we can turn their negative lesson into a positive one. Let's do that in the following exercise.

Exercise 2

The purpose of this exercise is to help you continue on a path of being a good student by showing you how to turn negative situations into positive lessons. Here are the directions for this exercise.

1. In the template below, make a list in the left-hand column of all the people who have made a negative impression on you from birth to present, were bad teachers, who hurt you, made you feel bad when you were around them, or had a negative impact of some sort on your life.

2. In the second column, write what they did and how they did it.

3. Ignore the third column for now.

People who have had a negative impact on me:	Why?	Affirmations

Now reflect on your list. Which of the seven principles were violated? Turn the negative lessons into a positive lesson by making a commitment that you'll never do to another person what this person has done to you. In column three, turn these into statements beginning with the words, "I will not . . . " followed by a second statement beginning with an affirmation of "I will . . . "

For example, if I wrote that my ex-boss was so "cynical, skeptical and critical of everything I ever said or did that it made me doubt myself," then in column three I would write, "**I will not** be cynical, skeptical, or critical of anyone. **I will** seek to understand, accept, and affirm everyone."

Notice the "I will" statement at the end. This helps to tie these affirmations back to the seven principles that we're now striving to exhibit in our interactions with others.

Complete this exercise, and then record all these new affirmations in your journal. Make them a part of your daily or weekly reflection and journaling activity. Reflect on the interactions you've had with others, and note how well you did exhibiting your affirmations and the seven principles. Make notes of areas where you need to improve, and focus on those areas in the coming day or week. Remember that success is a journey. Use your journal to chart your progress on your journey.

We'll focus our next exercise on the fact that we *are* on a journey. I've written in previous chapters that we're all moving toward the finest within us. We're moving at our own pace. And we're all driven by that same yearning. This exercise will help you examine what that means to you.

Exercise 3:

The purpose of this exercise is to help you begin to develop an awareness of your purpose, your reason for being here, your life vision. This exercise is designed to bring the dreams that may have been buried deep in your unconscious mind forward into your consciousness. Here are the directions for this exercise.

1. For this exercise, it might be helpful if you turn on some soothing music. For me it's helpful if the music is instrumental, with no distracting words sung in accompaniment.

2. Also remove as much visual stimuli as possible. Go into a room alone. Get the kids and pets out of the room. Remove all kinds of stimuli that would prompt your logical left brain to bring you back

to the confines of your present situation. Close the blinds. Dim the lights, or turn off all the lights and illuminate the room with a single candle.

3. Close your eyes and listen to the soothing music. Allow your body and mind to rest.

4. Now think about what you've read in this book about self-actualization and peak experiences. Slowly ask yourself these questions, and spend time reflecting on each one. (**Optional:** You may find that you benefit from having a trusted friend or family member read each of the following questions to you in a soft, soothing voice, allowing you to pause and reflect on each one, while you remain in your meditative state. Or you can try recording these questions in advance in your own voice then playing them back during your meditation, pausing appropriately between each question.)

- As you were reading the passages in this book about living the life you were born to live and being your one true self, what reflections did you have on your own life?

- What crossed your mind when you read about living the life you were born to live?

- What images flashed through your mind for yourself? What did you see yourself doing?

- If you mentally let go of your current situation and your perceived limitations, what could you see yourself doing? What do you dream about?

- What peak experiences have you had in your life that pointed to those things that can fulfill you most? What were you doing when you were your happiest?

- What were you born to do?

✏ Now open your eyes and write whatever you can imagine for yourself here.

Use pages in your journal if necessary to capture all your thoughts. You may want to record all this in your journal, so it can become part of your daily progress monitoring. Repeat this meditation exercise as often as you want or need in order to begin to see your life vision clearly.

Now let's reflect on what you wrote by answering these questions.

☞ Which of your current interests, jobs, activities, or relationships are moving you closer to the life you were born to live?

_____

_____

_____

_____

_____

_____

_____

_____

_____

_____

_____

_____

_____

Rhonda Jones

✐ Are any of your current interests, jobs, activities, or relationships moving you farther away from the life you were born to live?

_____

_____

_____

_____

_____

_____

_____

_____

_____

_____

_____

_____

_____

_____

_____

_____

✏ Write an action plan of steps you can take to (a) eliminate or manage those things in your life that could hinder your progress, and to (b) leverage those things that could move you closer to the ultimate goal of being who you were born to be:

_____

_____

_____

_____

_____

_____

_____

_____

_____

_____

_____

_____

_____

_____

_____

_____

_____

✎ Where are you in the journey?

_____

_____

_____

_____

_____

_____

_____

✎ What do you like about where you are?

_____

_____

_____

_____

_____

_____

_____

_____

✏ What would you like to change?

_____

_____

_____

_____

_____

_____

_____

✏ Who in your life is helping you on the journey? How?

_____

_____

_____

_____

_____

_____

_____

_____

_____

✏ Who do you know that could help you? How?

_____

_____

_____

_____

_____

_____

_____

✏ How can you help yourself?

_____

_____

_____

_____

_____

_____

_____

_____

Now that you have your action plan, reflect on it regularly and journal about your progress. If you discover that your dreams and aspirations are changing through this process, that's okay. Let your spirit lead you. You may never have thought about what it is you're born to do, so this will be a continual discovery process. You may learn that what you thought you wanted to do is changing through this process. Don't try to stop that from happening. Don't let your old mental models or paradigms govern you. Your one true self is inside trying to get out. These new realizations about yourself and what you want to do, occurring to you during this journaling, reflection, and growth period, are coming from your true purpose breaking down your old paradigms. Let that happen. Be open to it. Welcome it. It's an important part of the process.

It's okay if you find through your journaling that your intended destination and action plan to get there are changing. Trust your instincts and intuition, even if those closest to you do not. Remember, they only know the person who lives in your present cave. When you decide to move out of that cave, it disturbs the safe little world their left brain has concocted. Their natural response may be to try to put you back in the spot where they expect you to be. Understand and expect this response from others. Don't alienate them for having this predictable reaction. But don't let their reaction or pressure take precedence over your own inner voice.

As Thoreau said, "Move confidently in the direction of the life you have imagined." It's absolutely critical that you do this, not only for yourself, but for all of us. We're all connected. We're all teaching and learning from each other. We're either lifting each other up or tearing each other down. We're either helping each other up the mountain, or we're holding each other back.

Jung pointed out in his theory that we project onto others what we're unaware of in ourselves. If you feel like a failure, you'll project that cynicism onto those around you. You'll interact with them in a negative manner and pull them down with you. Therefore, even if it's uncomfortable for them to see you changing, it's in their best interest for you to move in the direction of the life you were born to live. If you're going to help others learn and grow . . . if you're going to lift others up . . . then you have to be progressing toward your own fulfillment. If you're stuck in one of the stages of development described by Erikson, then you not only can't get yourself to a higher level, you can't help others get there either . . . not your spouse . . . not your friends . . . not your kids . . . no one. You can't take others to a place you can't get to yourself. And, if you can't get there, you'll unconsciously resent or try to prevent the progress of others.

We're all here for a reason. We're all here to help each other reach fulfillment of that purpose. We're all teachers and students. But we can't teach others to do something that we can't teach ourselves. In order to be the best teacher we can be, we have to be continually progressing too. Being the teacher you could be requires perpetual movement toward the life you were born to live. It requires that you be constantly learning and growing. Being the best teacher you can be means that you must be a good student. So in this next exercise let's explore what kind of student you are.

Exercise 4:

The purpose of this exercise is to help you become aware of the kind of student you are, and to see opportunities in your own life where you can be more open to the lessons in everyday events. Here are the directions for the exercise.

1. Read the scenario and think about the situation it describes. You may be able to think of a real example from your own life that is very similar.

2. Reflect on the scenario provided, and on any similar real-life experience you've had. Ask yourself what you would think, feel, and/or do if you were actually in the situation described in the scenario. If you've had a similar experience, think about what you did in that situation and the thoughts and feelings you had during that time.

3. Briefly describe, in the space provided after each scenario, how you would think, feel, and act in this situation. Or, if you have had a similar experience, describe what you actually did in that situation.

4. Do not write how you would like to behave, but how you actually think you would instinctively react to the situation. Remember, this is an exercise designed to make us conscious of the good patterns we would like to emphasize and the not so good ones we want to improve. So don't judge yourself. Just be honest with yourself.

Scenario 1:

It's weird how fast time goes by. You can remember when you were the new whiz kid in the office. It seems as if overnight your hair has started to turn gray, and you're calling everyone "kid." Even more amazing is how much things have changed at work. When you started, there was no such thing as a personal computer. You can barely figure out how to limp along with the new e-mail system they're making you use. In the meantime, all these hotshot kids are doing everything on the computer . . . impressive analyses, slick charts, snazzy graphs, and professional reports. One of them even produced a report showing everything he thinks needs to be fixed in your department. Now the boss is asking why, with all your experience, didn't you think of these improvements. He didn't say it, but you got the distinct impression he thinks the times have passed you by.

☞ How would you react in this situation? What would you most likely think, feel, and do in this situation? Write your answer here.

_____

_____

_____

_____

_____

_____

_____

_____

_____

_____

_____

_____

One probable alternative is to have an immediate and uncontrollable reaction of disgust. It's not your fault you didn't have all this computer stuff when you were growing up. It's as second nature to these kids who grew up with it as using a pencil is to you. That's just the way it is. You can't be held responsible for the changing times. In fact, you're a victim of the changing times! What about all the time you've put in here? And, besides, you're dependable. These kids wander in and out at all hours on what they call "flex time." But you're never late, and you never leave early. Doesn't that count for anything? Go back to school? Why would you go back to school? You're fifty years old. You finished school a long time ago. If your boss wants you to know how to do that new stuff, he should teach you. Regardless, deep down you don't know why you need to be changing to something new. As long as somebody else knows how to do it, why do you need to learn anything new? What's wrong with how you are now? It used to be good enough, back when you were the young whiz kid. Why does management have it in for all the older employees?

Here's another possible reaction. You're not surprised that the boss is impressed by the analysis done by your young colleague. You were impressed by it too. You have to admit, these kids and the things they can do are amazing. You think, if there was a way to combine their state of the art capabilities with your experience and business savvy, what a winning combination that would be. Congratulating your young coworker on the fine analysis he performed, you begin asking him questions about how he did it, to see what you can learn. As you listen to him, you remember your own youthful exuberance at his age. How did you let yourself get so complacent, you wonder? Seeing the power of the computer programs he's using inspires you. It's been a long time since you went to school. But you feel pretty sure, with your determination and his coaching, you can pick this up pretty quickly. You'll have to do it on your own time. But you'll be able to use these new skills in so many aspects of your life. It will be worth it.

What's the difference between these two responses to the scenario? This lesson is about taking responsibility for your own learning and growth. In the first response, the person is engaging in victim mentality. They're a victim of the changing times, a victim of the hotshot kid in the office, a victim of their inappreciative boss . . . they are just "poor me." They've long ago stopped feeling responsible for or taking initiative for their own growth. They feel if they must be forced to learn something in order to keep their job, then the boss should be responsible for spoon-feeding it to them. This mentality virtually guarantees that a person won't learn anything, even if the boss does provide the instruction. They've already rejected the notion that learning is of value "at their age." They prefer instead to just spend their time engaging in self-pity.

In the second reaction, on the other hand, this person is taking responsibility. They demonstrate a healthy response. While this scenario suggests they may have fallen behind briefly, due to a lapse of some kind, they're exhibiting the attitude and behavior of a life-long learner. They recognize that ultimately the responsibility for fulfilling their potential rests with none other than themselves. They also realize that opportunities to learn abound, including being coached by a younger colleague. The person in option two is displaying the responsibility and accountability that makes one an excellent student. They're recognizing the opportunity in a regular, everyday event to learn from the teachers around them.

Review your response to the scenario. On which end of the spectrum are you when it comes to being responsible for your own learning? Are you accepting responsibility for your own continual growth? Do you see these kinds of situations as opportunities? Taking responsibility for our own learning and growth, and not being jealous or intimidated by those who might teach us, is a critical behavior for being a good student.

Scenario 2:

The planned unit development neighborhood you live in has been a good place to live. Most of the neighbors are friendly, and some are even willing to go the extra mile when helping hands are needed to keep the place in order. The only issue has been the developer who is continuing to build condos in the neighborhood. He has left materials piled up to the point that termites have been attracted, and the mounds of excavated dirt now have weeds towering all over them. Perhaps the worst thing is the old rusty equipment he leaves parked right at the gated entrance.

A homeowner's association should be formed to challenge the developer's habits, which are surely decreasing the property values. Everyone in the neighborhood agrees on this point, but no one seems to have the courage or experience to take the lead, pull the association together, and be the inaugural president. You have some very definite opinions about what needs to be done in the neighborhood, and you have a strong desire to see the situation improved.

You're also popular and acquainted with many of your neighbors. But you've never been the kind of person others would describe as a leader. In fact, you've never held any kind of leadership position at all.

✏ How would you react in this situation? What would you most likely think, feel, and do in this situation? Write your answer here.

_____

_____

_____

_____

_____

_____

_____

_____

_____

_____

_____

_____

_____

_____

_____

_____

Here's one possible response. Sure, you've been very vocal to your neighbors about what should be done. You did that because you were hoping one of them would step up and do something about it. How could they expect you to lead something like this? You don't have any experience in matters like these. You feel sure you'd be more likely to make so many mistakes that the situation would only deteriorate. You're more than willing to stand behind the leader, whoever it may be, but you just wouldn't feel comfortable trying to do something like this that you've never done before. The most you can do is just keep talking to your neighbors, and keep it stirred up, until some of the more qualified people in the neighborhood finally decide to take charge.

That's a likely response to the situation. Now consider this one. You survey your population of neighbors. Many are retirees. They have the free time available to take on some of these neighborhood issues and projects. But you have to admit, in most cases, they don't have the temperament. They're either too irritable and abrasive, too nervous, or too complacent to really provide the kind of leadership that could be effective in this situation. Many who are not retired are too busy with work and family. While they share your concern and desire to bring about improvements, and probably have the relevant experience, they simply don't have the time to lead the initiative. Plus, because they're so busy, they probably haven't had the time to get to know as many of the neighbors as you have.

You're the only logical choice. All you lack is experience, and the only way you're going to get it is to give this a shot. You'll just have to find some people who have done this before, ask them for pointers, round up some willing volunteers to prop you up where you're weak, learn from your mistakes, and figure it out as you go.

What's the big difference between the first and second reaction to this scenario? In option one, there's no opportunity for learning, because there is no risktaking. The attitude of the "student" in option one is that learning is static. All the learning and experience that can be gained has already been gained. The cup is already full and no new contents can be added. So anything not already in the repertoire can't be acquired. This person inhibits their own learning by being afraid to try something new for fear of making mistakes.

The student in option two, on the other hand, recognizes that he or she probably will make mistakes, but that this is the only way to learn. This student is open to learning because he or she is willing to risk making mistakes. This willingness to step outside his or her comfort zone and take a chance creates a dynamic and ongoing stream of learning opportunities.

Now review your response to the scenario. To what end of that spectrum do you lean? Are you willing to risk struggling at times, having failed attempts, or making mistakes in order to learn to do something new? A truly good student is willing to take that chance.

Scenario 3:

You've volunteered to go with a group from where you work to help build a Habitat for Humanity house. You've never before volunteered to do anything so large and charitable for someone else, which is part of your rationale for doing it now. You believe it's important to have all kinds of experiences in order to continue learning and growing. Besides, this project is right down your alley. You're a take charge kind of person, who's really goal-oriented. If the goal today is to get this house under roof, you're going to let nothing stand in your way of doing just that.

When you arrived at the job site this morning, you noticed some new faces—some from work, some from the Habitat for Humanity organization, and you don't know who the rest of them are. Throughout the day it has been a lot of volunteers to coordinate. On the one hand, you're glad to see so many volunteers because you knew it would be a big job to get this house framed and under roof in one day. On the other hand, it's been exasperating. So many people don't know what they're doing. They don't seem to be there to actually help build the house. This is like a social gathering for them. There's one guy who just acts like a big cheerleader.

✏ Try to put yourself in this person's shoes. Have you ever been in a situation like this before? What happened? How could you imagine this scenario continuing to unfold? How would you most likely behave during this day? Write your answer here.

_____

_____

_____

_____

_____

_____

_____

_____

_____

_____

_____

_____

_____

Here's one possible conclusion to the scenario. You find yourself wanting to just tell people what to do. Can't they see what needs to be done? What about that big, strong man who keeps clowning around? He could really handle some heavy work if he'd just get serious and focus his efforts on the task at hand. You wonder if he's totally oblivious to the fact that you're trying to build a house here. You realize that you've been in situations like this over and over in your life. You always seem to end up having to work harder and carry more than your share of the load because others can't stay focused on meeting the objective. You double your efforts and try to make up for everyone else. At the end of the day, what you've learned most from this experience is how difficult it is to frame a house with a bunch of inexperienced volunteers!

Now here's another possible conclusion. From the moment you arrive at the job site, you are in awe. There are so many different people there to help. The staff and volunteer crew leaders from the Habitat organization are fascinating. You learn they're from all walks of life. One is an older southern-gentleman attorney who reminds you of someone straight from a John Grisham novel. He's been volunteering as a crew leader for over eleven years and has lost count of how many homes he has helped build. Another is a doctor, and he's riding the biggest Harley-Davidson motorcycle you've ever seen.

Whoever thinks that doctors spend all their free time on the golf course should see this guy go at it on this house.

Your attention wanders from one interesting person to another. From the building site supervisor, who comes across as a tough old bird on the outside but flashes sparkling blue eyes from underneath his bushy, white eyebrows, to the soft-spoken director of the Habitat organization, who gave the grateful welcome address at the start of the day, to the kind little ladies from the Methodist Church who supplied lunch, to the humble single mother of three for whom the house is being built, to the members of the second volunteer team that showed up to take your place in the afternoon, you are moved, impressed, and inspired many times over and over throughout the day.

There's this one crew leader named Lewis, who seems like a big cheerleader. His mission today appears to be to minister to everyone's spirit and to make sure everyone is happy and having a good time. At one point you notice Lewis helping a young man install a window. The young man is partially handicapped and working painfully slow. He struggles to use the tape measure, to help maneuver the window into position, to handle the hammer and hang onto the nails in his feeble hands. His work is slow and painstaking, but Lewis is patient, helpful, and encouraging. With great determination and effort, the young man finally stands back with pride to survey the completed job. He beams with the joy of having done something he has never done before . . . perhaps something that people have been telling him all this life he's not capable of doing.

You realize, as you look at Lewis and the young stranger, standing with their arms around each other's shoulders, that this is what this volunteer activity is all about. It's not about getting the house under roof today. In fact, you realize that you probably won't achieve that goal. That's really not what is most important today. That's the lesson you'll take away from this volunteer experience. Giving of yourself to help others is not about just finishing the task. It's about the process by which you finish the task. It's not about the "what." It's about the "how." You learned far more than how to build a house on this volunteer mission today. More importantly, you learned how to live your life.

This scenario is about increasing your sensitivity to the lessons that are presented to you as a "student," all the time, in every situation. What's the difference between these two responses to the scenario? In the first response, there's little to no awareness of such lessons. The person is so overly focused on the obvious objective of building the house, that there's literally no room for anything else. Despite the fact that people from all walks of life have been united by this project—people from a wide range of national origins, race, background, and with a broad spectrum of talents, interests, and experiences—there's no awareness of the opportunity to learn from them, nor is there an attempt to do so. It's as if the person in option one is wearing their dogged goal-orientation like a suit of armor that limits their field of vision to straight ahead, deflecting anything and everything around them. They may drive a lot of nails, more than anyone else, perhaps. But by the end of the day, all they will have learned is how to drive a nail.

The person in option two, on the other hand, is exhibiting a high sensitivity to the lessons around them. Sure, they're learning to drive nails, frame walls, and install windows—something they've never done before—but more importantly, they're learning deeper, more meaningful lessons from those around them. From the beginning of the day, it's obvious this person recognized the great opportunity presented to them in the company of so many diverse individuals. They are actively seeking to learn about the other people and looking for something amazing in each and every one. They are working on the job at hand, but they never stop watching for the lessons. They listen, watch, and marvel at the tiny miracles occurring over and over throughout the day. At the end of the day, they've learned something far more important than how to drive a nail. They've learned how to help others, and how much that lifts us all in return.

This heightened sensitivity to the lessons is a skill that can be developed, and once developed, perpetuates itself. Once you become focused on this amazing side of life, you'll notice more and more the life-changing lessons of the everyday. Which end of the spectrum are you on? Do you need to increase your sensitivity to the lessons? Good students are always cultivating this ability and always on the lookout for the life-changing lessons in everyday events.

Scenario 4:

This morning you had the opportunity to hear a young man speak about working with the poor in Central America. Never having the opportunity or even the desire, you've barely traveled outside your state lines. You've seen some of the rare news coverage, but this is the first time you've ever met someone who has actually been there and been immersed in the local culture. He has spoken of the people he met there and their great need. He says they're good, hardworking people who desperately need our help. You know this young man. He grew up here in your community. Your family went to church with his family every Sunday. Your kids went to school with him. He married your daughter's best friend from school, and they now have two children, three and four years old. The entire family goes on these mission trips together.

☞ How would you react in this situation? What would you most likely think, feel, and do in this situation? Write your answer here.

_____

_____

_____

_____

_____

_____

_____

_____

_____

_____

_____

_____

_____

_____

_____

_____

One reaction you might have is that you've heard people like this young man speak before. They're all a little too oversentimental in your opinion. It doesn't matter what this kid thinks. He'll just have to learn the hard way that those people can't be helped. They're in that situation because they don't have enough sense to get out of it. It's the same as the situation around here. You can build those people houses and before you know it, they've knocked the windows out of them. This kid was just wasting his time down there, when he could've been up here doing something productive. You've known for a long time that these bleeding heart sentimentalists are just wasting everybody's time and money. You know this kid and his family. You never thought they lacked so much common sense. He should stop dragging his young family through these undeveloped countries, get a real job, and give them a good home. How is he ever going to provide for those children? You're surprised that his parents act so proud of him.

Now here's another possible reaction. Something about what this young man is saying interests you. It's true you've never really supported this kind of mission work. You've believed it was like casting pearls before the swine. That's what you always heard from your parents. How could those backward heathens know how to use and preserve any of our wealth we might share with them? But this young man has actually been there. And you know him . . . know his family. He's a smart kid who left a very lucrative job to go down there and work. He's so articulate on the subject and so sincere. As you listen to him calling these people by name and telling their story, you begin for the first time to see them as real people just like yourself. You realize that you and those you learned from may have been wrong all along. As you begin to listen to the young man's heartfelt words, you begin to think maybe, just maybe, you've been wrong about it. After all, you've never been there, and he has. Following his speech, you ask him to come over and talk one-on-one. And this time you listen . . . really listen.

What's the difference between these two responses to the scenario? This scenario is about being the kind of student who listens to points of view that are different from your own and that challenge your old paradigms. It's easy to fall into the kind of trap where you don't accept differing points of view, especially when your dinosaur left brain is working overtime to package everything up and get a handle on all of it. Admitting that we don't know where we stand on something or that our position might be wrong is an insecure place to be. So, like the person in option one, we decide how we feel about a situation even when we have no direct, firsthand experience. Then our positions, our paradigms, become so hardened we don't even allow them to be challenged, no matter how compelling and accurate the challenge may be. Like the person in option one, we can become almost belligerent in our self-defense in order to avoid the slightest feeling of insecurity born of lack of experience or knowledge.

Conversely, in option two, the person is carefully allowing his or her paradigms to be challenged. They're questioning the source of their existing mental model and allowing room to consider an alternative. They're listening, really listening, not just with their ears. They're doing more than just hearing. They're allowing this new information to sink into their thoughts and their hearts. They're seeking to learn more that might eventually allow them to create a new, more enlightened opinion. This student in option two is listening, opening up, and challenging their paradigms in order to keep growing personally. Do you fall on this end of the spectrum? This person is exhibiting the behaviors that will make one a good lifelong student.

Scenario 5:

You signed up for this artist's workshop because deep down inside you've always known you were born to be an artist. Your first job was in an advertising agency. You were just a young administrative assistant, but you were around creative, artistic people all day, and you loved it. Then the kids came. Soon thereafter your husband's aging parents moved in with you. The resulting communal lifestyle, with husband, kids, unhealthy in-laws, and even the dogs placing demands on you, has robbed you of all your time for any artistic expression. But now here you are in this class listening to the instructor explain how you can make this a part of your busy lifestyle. That's his specialty—teaching people how to make time for, connect with, and release the artist within. The workshop had sounded so compelling, and now his words are even more so. There's even a busy corporate executive here, who has managed to work enough time into his schedule to write a book using the system being taught in this workshop.

✏ Try to put yourself in this person's shoes. How could you imagine this scenario continuing to unfold? How would you most likely behave during this day? Write your answer here.

_____

_____

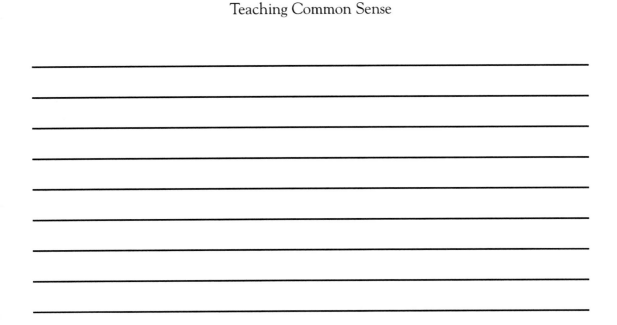

Here's one possible reaction. You hear everything the instructor is saying. But how can you possibly exercise this on a daily basis? You barely made it to this workshop. You even had to bring your youngest son with you and arrange for your sister to come by and pick him up on her way home from work. You really want to do this. You always have. And you think you have some good ideas. But your life is just too hectic to fit this in right now. Everyone needs and expects so much from you. You can't stop thinking about what you have to do when you get home long enough to really engage in the workshop exercises. Maybe that busy businessman wrote a book. But he's single with no children. So is the instructor of the workshop. What do they know about making time for yourself in a busy family like yours? You've struggled through two days of this workshop, and all you've accomplished is getting two days behind on your chores at home. There's no point in coming back for the third and final day. You've just wasted your money. For you, this is going to have to wait until the kids are grown, and you're not taking care of elderly family members, and you don't have so much house to clean . . .

Well, that's an understandable reaction of a busy mother. Now here's another possible reaction. This workshop is making you a nervous wreck. It's as if the instructor is speaking directly to all your hopes and fears. Listening to him is like listening to an evangelist. You feel unanimously convicted of all the ways you've undermined yourself over the years. When was it exactly that you stopped attending to your own personal learning and growth? How long has it been since you really made any progress toward being the person you were born to be? How could your family say they love you and not support you in that quest?

The problem is, you realize, that you've never asked for their support and made an earnest attempt to do this. Instead, you've trained them to consume all your time and energy. The instructor insists that your family can and will adapt and give you the support you need. When they start to see the happy, fulfilled person who emerges, when you really start becoming your one true self, it will be contagious. What better lesson to give your children than to see you fulfilling your purpose and becoming the person you were born to be? Your husband agreed to do the cooking for you this weekend. And your sister agreed to keep your young son, so you could attend this workshop. Maybe you could do this.

The instructor is asking you to trust him and his system to help you become the person you were born to be. He believes in you, even though you don't believe in yourself yet, and he has many success stories to back up that belief. You're nervous and apprehensive about making this change in your lifestyle. But the instructor has no reason to mislead you. He simply wants to help you do what you were born to do. You decide to trust him and give it a try. Tonight, when you get home, you'll talk to your family about how you can carve out a few minutes of your day for yourself.

This scenario is about trusting the teachers who come into our lives and the lessons they bring us versus being cynical and skeptical and, thus, closed to the messages. What's the difference between these two reactions to this scenario? In the first option, the woman is overcome by cynicism and skepticism. Even though she wants what the workshop is offering her, she's unable to set aside those negative thoughts and feelings. She's unable to see that just the sheer fact she made time in her busy schedule to be here this weekend is proof she can create the necessary time and space in her life. She's still more comfortable feeling sorry for herself, making excuses, and complaining . . . a familiar pattern that has already prevented her for many years from making any progress toward living the life she was born to live. How ironic. She's more comfortable in this uncomfortable yet familiar comfort zone than she is stepping out of that box.

On the other hand, in option two she's able to trust, at least long enough to listen and make an attempt. The instructor's belief in his students is enough to make her trust. Rather than trying to figure out why he's encouraging her and what angle he could possibly be working, she instead notices the sincerity in his approach. She not only hears, but also sees the success stories with her own eyes in her other classmates. This student in option two learns because she sets aside any feelings of cynicism or skepticism and allows herself to trust her teacher—the person who knows—who has done it and seen it work. The student in option two is exhibiting the good student behavior of trusting the teacher and giving the lesson a chance to change her life for the better. How about you? Are you the kind of student that is willing to trust the teacher?

Scenario 6:

Times have been hard before, but you're not quite sure they've ever been this bad. Being a single mother is almost as difficult as raising kids in a bad marriage. Divorcing the children's father certainly didn't make parenthood any easier. If anything, it made it harder. You'll always have to deal with him where the children are concerned—a fact that's complicated by his lack of willingness to provide for his children.

It's not enough that you get no help from this deadbeat dad, you're not getting any help from anywhere. It seems like every small step you make forward financially, the government eats it all up in taxes. And the never-ending cost of paying the mortgage and utilities and the basic necessities of maintenance on the house and car seems to grow increasingly burdensome. Now, to top it all off, your company has announced it's downsizing. Your job is being eliminated in eight months, and your severance will run out two and a half months after that.

✏ How would you react in this situation? What would you most likely think, feel, and do in this situation? Write your answer here.

_____

_____

_____

_____

_____

_____

_____

_____

_____

_____

_____

_____

_____

Unfortunately, this is an all too familiar situation in our society today, and one of the possible responses is equally familiar. Why should you be surprised, you think? This was bound to happen. Life is hard and then you die, right? You don't even know why you try. If the government or big business doesn't get you, some worthless con artist like your ex-husband will. There's no point in trying to better yourself. You would only be making yourself a bigger target for all those untrustworthy men out there looking for a woman to take care of them. Besides, the higher you climb means you have farther to fall, and it's going to be even more painful when you hit the bottom. What's the use? You'll never find another job as good as this one around here. It's not like it was anybody's dream job, but it had decent pay and benefits. You might as well just sell the house now, cut your losses, and move back in with your mother. There's no point in trying anymore. Someone is always out to get you. If the government wants to take so much of your hard-earned money in taxes, then they can just spend some of it to take care of you and your kids.

Here's another possible reaction. This latest news from your employer was definitely shocking. You've known for years that the company was struggling in this area, but you never imagined that this major downsizing might be the eventual outcome. At first, you felt a little panic creep in. The children's father has displayed an inability to provide for their needs. There's no reason to believe he'll be any real help in this situation. And you were barely scraping by. Still, you're determined to figure this out. You've survived tough times before. You'll weather this storm too.

You've been going to all the sessions with the placement agency that the company has provided to help people through the separation transition. They've helped so many others like you through these situations. The man teaching the class has been through three corporate downsizings himself. He has shown encouraging statistics about how the majority of those affected by a staff reduction like this almost always end up in a better situation. And he's living proof of that fact. You quickly force those panicked thoughts from your mind and start focusing on the future. What did you always want to do, but never gave it a try? What steps could you take now to begin doing something that would not only support your family, but also make you happy in the process? This might actually be fun, you tell yourself, and you have a whole ten months to work on it. You throw yourself into the transition team activities.

What's the difference between these two responses to this scenario? This scenario is about being an optimist and having faith in the possibilities rather than being a pessimist. It's the old glass half full or half empty analogy. The person in option one is exhibiting the negative behavior of a pessimist. The glass is half empty and getting more empty all the time. This person believes this inevitable trend will continue, regardless of what she does. The pessimist not only closes themselves off to the possibilities; they also create their own self-fulfilling prophecy. The pessimist convinces themselves that the situation can only get worse and that they should give up. Then once they give up, of course, it gets worse. So they pat themselves on the back and say, "See, I was right." And this never-ending negative pattern, which can only yield negative consequences, is set.

On the flip side, the person in the second response is exhibiting optimistic behaviors, and she, too, is creating a self-fulfilling prophecy. Her optimism is allowing her to be open to the lessons and possibilities around her. Her optimism and faith in the possibilities is freeing her imagination and creativity to dream and then to take steps toward her dreams. The optimist can be helped because they believe in the possibilities. They have faith. The student who is an optimist can be taught. The optimistic student sees each bump in the road, each challenge, as opportunities to learn and grow. What doesn't kill you will make you stronger. That's the optimist's battle cry. The good student is an optimist who has faith in *what could be*, regardless of *what is*. Which kind of student are you?

How did you do on the scenarios in this exercise? Let's recap the good student behaviors depicted.

Good Learner Behaviors

- Accept Responsibility and be accountable for your lifelong learning.
- Risk making mistakes in order to take advantage of all learning opportunities.
- Notice and be sensitive to the lessons all around you every day.
- Challenge your opinions and mindsets and the basis for your paradigms, and allow yourself to consider new and different points of view.
- Trust those placed in your life to be your teacher, and be open to the help they provide for your continual development.
- Have faith in the possibilities for your future, and turn every obstacle into an opportunity to learn and grow.

Remember, we said at the beginning of this exercise that all humanity is dependent upon each of us being good teachers to help each other reach fulfillment. And being a good teacher—the best teacher you could be—requires that you be a good student. You need to be a good student so that you're always progressing toward your own personal fulfillment. Your reaching the mountaintop is what allows you to take others there. That's what makes it possible for you to be a good teacher. This is what Gibran was referring to in his proverb about a teacher: "Whoever would be a teacher of men let him begin by teaching himself before teaching others . . ."

How are you doing? What kind of student are you? What are you teaching yourself? Are you taking responsibility for your own learning and growth? Are you willing to risk making mistakes and try something new, so you can learn from those experiences? Have you worked at developing an increased sensitivity to the lessons all around you each day? Have you developed the awareness to enable yourself to be open to the continual stream of learning and growth opportunities presented to you? Are you able to trust others who have accomplished something that you would like to do? Do you set aside your feelings of cynicism, doubt, and skepticism to let these teachers guide you? Are you capable of listening, not only to what others are trying to share with you, but also to your own voice, in order to recognize when you are being governed by an old, limiting paradigm? Can you let go of what you thought you knew and allow your old positions to be challenged? Can you make room for knowledge that's new and different? Are you an optimist who believes in the possibilities? Are you able to strive to turn the bleakest of situations into an opportunity to learn and grow?

Take responsibility for your own continual growth. Take risks and learn from mistakes. Be sensitive and open to all the lessons, even in seemingly insignificant everyday events. Trust the good teachers in your life. Really listen and constantly challenge your paradigms. Have faith in the possibilities. These are the behaviors and attitudes that make you a good student. These are the choices that yield positive natural consequences. These create a positive self-fulfilling prophecy. These behaviors and attitudes, by definition, will make you the best teacher you possibly could be. People need models more than they need critics. When you model these *good student behaviors*, you'll be a good teacher.

Spend a few minutes reflecting on what you've learned from this exercise. Which scenario struck a chord with you? Which one carried the biggest lesson for you? Make a few notes about it in the space provided below, and spend some time writing in your journal about it. What did you learn *about yourself?* What would you like to work on?

_____

_____

_____

_____

_____

_____

_____

For the final exercise in this chapter, we'll return to the seven principles. The seven principles encompass all the elements for being an effective teacher that have been described in this book. Living by the seven principles, by definition, means that you're delivering high levels of human nourishment, and you're also exhibiting good student behaviors and attitudes. By focusing on the seven principles, you can and will make noticeable progress toward being the person you were born to be, *and* you'll be helping all those around you too. So, for this exercise, we're going to refer back to the seven principles checklist.

Exercise 5:

The goal of this last exercise is two-fold. First, we want to increase your awareness of and focus on how well you are exhibiting the seven principles on a daily basis with everyone in your circle of influence. Second, we want to identify which of the seven principles is closely aligned with your strengths, how you can maximize and leverage those, and how you can manage the areas that are not your strengths. Here are the directions for the exercise.

1. Review the seven principles checklist below. Now refer to your list of personal attributes and qualities (Exercise 4 in Chapter 5, page 176).

2. With which of the seven principles do you think your strengths are closely aligned? Using the template provided below, write in the second column how your strengths align with the principles.

3. In the third column, write the evidence in your life of this alignment. Whom, by name, have you helped or taught by exhibiting this behavior? When did you do it, and what, specifically, was the result?

4. If you can't produce these specific examples, then there's no direct evidence that you're already exhibiting this principle. It may be to some degree aligned with your strengths, and it may be something you aspire to be good at. But, if you can't definitely say that you have done it, then you can't claim it yet. So be fair with yourself, and complete columns two and three. Remember, this is just for you, and there are no right or wrong answers. We're going to turn this into a good growth exercise, which will be explained after you've finished completing columns two and three.

Seven Principles Checklist:	How my strengths align with this principle:	Evidence/Examples of how this is my strengh:
Give Unconditional Love and Acceptance • Focus on seeing the unique qualities and beauty in every person you meet. • Speak kindly and nonjudgmentally. Look for ways to affirm the other person. • Accept each person as they are. Look beyond a person's actions and focus on loving the soul of the person. • Respect each person's right to be who they are, feel what they feel, and think what they think. Search for commonality versus difference.		
Be Structured and Organized • Remember that the dinosaur brain is naturally searching for safety, and that the structure and organization are good for all situations. • Give the other person's left brain a reason to trust what you're saying or demonstrating. • Recognize that the left and right brain will always be fighting to take the lead. Expect this unpredictability and don't let it cause you to deviate from your facilitave approach.		

Seven Principles Checklist:	How my strengths align with this principle:	Evidence/Examples of how this is my strengh:
• Focus on creating an environment that enables the dinosaur brain to rest and allows the creative right brain to soar.		
Be Committed to a Vision • Focus not on how things have been or how things are, but rather on how things could be. • Focus on how you can assist by removing barriers. • Be willing to go the distance. Put forth the effort, and do all that you can do. • Broaden your focus beyond yourself or those closest to you. Envision a better future that encompasses all creation and work every day to make that vision a reality.		
Be Inspiring • Realize how difficult it is for humans to see beyond existing paradigms, and deliver a consistently high level of energy that dissolves those hardened barriers. • Question the assumptions on which the desire to hold on to the old is based. Help them make the choice to let some of it go, so something new might take its place.		

Seven Principles Checklist:	How my strengths align with this principle:	Evidence/Examples of how this is my strengh:
• Live by a "we can do it" attitude. Inspire them to take the first step into something new by taking that first step with them. • Paint a mental picture of the possibilities, and become a living reminder of those possibilities.		
<u>Make a Connection</u> • Maintain an outward focus on others versus an inward focus on yourself. • Make it a priority to get to know others as individuals and recognize the needs they are expressing both verbally and nonverbally. • Start from where they are, not from where you think they should or could be. • Focus on how you can use your energy to lift each person you encounter.		
<u>Believe in Others</u> • Remove the words "no," "don't," and "can't," from your vocabulary. Replace them with an "anything is possible" attitude. • Respect others' rights and abilities to make choices. Trust that you are playing your important part in their journey by simply believing in them.		

Seven Principles Checklist:	How my strengths align with this principle:	Evidence/Examples of how this is my strengh:
• Realize that those you encounter possess the ability within to find the answers they need to be all they were born to be. • Ignore feelings of uncertainty, insecurity, or doubt. Act on your intuition—the message you're meant to deliever to others—and give each individual the most and absolute best you have to offer. Believe that this is a part of the reason you're here.		
<u>Be a Coach and Lifelong Learner</u> • Remember that others are watching. Attend to your own development and behavior. Model the standards you believe in. • Create an environment in which every attempt at something new is an opportunity to learn. Turn mistakes into growth and successes into rewards. • Nurture a sense of pride. Find something to celebrate in each individual's effort. • Remember that what you give to others creates a reciprocal relationship, returning multiplied to you, so that you are continuously learning and growing too.		

Good job! You've taken a big first step. You've claimed your strengths and identified how they enable you to exhibit the seven principles. You don't have to be humble or pretend that you don't have strengths. They're your gift . . . your inner genius. You should be proud of them.

Likewise, you've admitted a true fact of being human. It's okay not to be the best at everything. You've identified and admitted the areas in which you are weakest. Now you can really begin to soar. Now you can work at doing more of what you do best, while being aware of what might bite you . . . improving what you can . . . and being careful to manage the rest.

We're going to use your journal as the tool for practicing the seven principles. Our goal with this ongoing daily or weekly practice is to be intentional about the review and practice of the principles. We'll always keep in mind that the ultimate goal is to excel with your strengths and manage your weaknesses. So be sure not to set up practice for yourself that is only aimed at fixing your weaknesses. That's not where we want our focus to be. The focus will always be on exhibiting the seven principles to the best of your personal ability . . . being the best you possibly can be at all seven. Here are the directions for your regular journaling activity.

Regular Journaling Activity

1. Record in your journal the principles that are your strengths, as well as those that are not strengths.

2. Establish a daily or weekly routine for spending time reflecting on your personal growth through this journaling work.

3. Depending on which interval you choose, at the beginning of the day or at the beginning of the week, spend time deciding which of the seven principles will be your focus for that time period. Choose only one principle on which to focus for that day or week.

4. Think ahead about what opportunities you may have to practice it. Who is likely to be in your circle of influence? In what kind of setting? How might you exhibit this principle toward these individuals? Think in terms of specifics. What specific things might you say to them or do for them in order to deliver the principle you're practicing? What are the things you've said or done in the past that you

want to make a conscious effort to repeat . . . or to avoid . . . in order to exhibit this principle to the best of your ability. If the principle selected is not one of your strengths, make sure you're setting realistic goals.

5. Record in your journal the principle you're going to practice and your action plan. Try to keep these goals and plans in focus throughout your practice day or week time period.

6. At the end of your practice period, record in your journal how you did. What opportunities did you have to practice the principle? What was the situation? Who was involved in the interaction? What did you do? What was the result? Do you think your actions had a positive impact on others? How did it make you feel? What did you learn? What do you want to try the next time you're focused on practicing this principle?

7. Now think again about all those with whom you interacted during your practice period, both those people you know personally and those you don't know. Did you take advantage of every opportunity presented to you? Did you just practice delivering the principle to those you know and ignore those you don't know? Did you find it easier to practice with strangers than with those closest to you? Can you identify some patterns that have developed in your interactions with those who are closest to you, which are counter to the principle you were practicing? Think about how you can break those destructive patterns and begin to routinely exhibit the positive behaviors associated with the seven principles. Record your action plan in your journal, and refer back to it the next time you choose this principle to practice.

Rotate through the seven principles, intentionally practicing one at a time on a regular daily or weekly interval. Be diligent about your practice; remain positive; and be fair with yourself. Learning to live by the seven principles isn't a sprint. It's a marathon, and you don't win a marathon in the first one hundred meters. Success comes from weathering the challenges and continually learning and growing, one step at a time.

As you continue your practice, rotating through the seven principles, note your progress in your journal. Are your strengths really aligned with the principles that you initially thought they were? Were you correct about your weaknesses? Have you discovered strengths you didn't know you had? Have you recognized blind spots that you need to actively manage?

Eventually, you will find that exhibiting all seven principles will become second nature. You **will** excel with your strengths. And when you do, we'll all be better off as a result.

The Universal Cure

By learning you will teach; by teaching you will learn.

– Latin Proverb

Seven

This book grew, innocently enough, out of a single focus group comment. The question, "What must I do to be a teacher?" not only struck a nerve, it haunted me. Is it really rocket science? I wondered. Did I actually learn something in that adult education Master's program that suddenly flipped a switch inside and turned me on as a teacher? Or did I already possess knowledge that was merely organized and refined by the experience of the Master's program? Of course, I finally realized that was it. I was already teaching informally every day. I had learned how to do it from the continual stream of teachers who had passed through my life—teachers both good and bad—teaching me those necessary commonsense principles. Those life lessons shaped me. I was sure of it.

But the focus group comment had made me realize another fact. Not everyone sees the continual stream of lessons in their life. Not everyone recognizes their great teachers. Not everyone converts those lessons—good and bad—into the life-shaping guides they are intended to be. Unlike me, some people don't even learn the hard way. Some people never learn.

Once I became aware of that fact, I realized this book is not just for people who want to be professional teachers. Some of my greatest teachers—Lynn, Ken, Gordon, and Tom—are not schoolteachers at all. They're friends, coworkers, managers, and neighbors. It's for people like them that this book was written. It's for parents, single people, married couples, everyone . . . and, yes, teachers too. This book is for anyone who teaches, and that excludes no one.

We all possess the natural abilities, which only need to be cultivated and exercised, to be successful teachers in pursuit of our collective purpose. Each moment defines our success in this life. Every step is a part of that journey. Even my attempt to write in this book about that process has been filled with life-enhancing learning for me. Therefore, my belief is redoubled in the power of this message for everyone.

We all have a unique potential to fulfill in this life, which is part of a larger, all-encompassing purpose. We have a dinosaur brain, which in an attempt to protect us guides us into limiting perspectives. But we're also blessed with an innate ability to overcome those self-imposed barriers. We have the ability to learn from and through our experiences and our interactions with others, in order to be all that we were born to be.

239

Therefore, part of the reason we're here is to be good teachers—to understand how difficult this lifelong evolution can be toward fulfilling our purpose for being here, and to nurture that process for all with whom we interact. We become good teachers by being good students who recognize the teachers and lessons in our own lives, which are intended to expand our consciousness and assist in our lifelong learning process. Underneath all the noise and trappings of society, we're all connected. We can all grow together and have those peak experiences together . . . or not. It's our choice. Choosing to be the best student and teacher you can be, following the seven commonsense principles described in this book, is choosing to live the life you were born to live. When you apply these seven principles to teach others to be all they can be, that's when you'll finally come to know yourself.

It's like this. If I thought I had the cure for cancer, after so many friends and family members being impacted by it, I would be willing to risk everything—I would fight through any obstacle—to bring that cure to the world. That's how I feel about these seven principles. That's why I wrote this book.

Too many people I see are missing something. Too many of those I encounter are aimlessly floating from one diversion to another. It's a disease that plagues all humanity, and too many people will die from this disease without ever living the life they were born to live. I, for one, can't sit idly by and watch all that potential being wasted.

Alone we can do so little.
Together we can do so much.
– Helen Keller

The *great philosopher* Charlie Brown said, "Saying you have potential means you haven't done anything yet." That's not my point. In this case, seeing potential is the same as seeing the future. I see a bright future in which every person is intentional about helping one another learn and grow to be all they can be . . . to be their one true self.

It won't always be easy. Many obstacles remain. It's a journey for which there is no one map. Each individual must chart his or her own way. I've heard it described as stepping into the fog with only a compass to guide you. Along the way, you may have limited visibility. You may wander into a box canyon and have to retrace your steps, or stumble into a ravine and have to construct a bridge. It may be a difficult journey, wandering through the fog without a map. But along the way you will encounter markers that help you know you're on track—those great teachers who enable your journey. And you always have your compass. The seven principles described in this book are your compass. Trust them and they will keep you always pointed toward the mountaintop—your ultimate destination.

On a walk through the woods on a fog-enshrouded morning two days after Thanksgiving, I encountered a wild turkey. Obviously pardoned from the Thanksgiving dinner table, he was busily scratching the bed of fallen leaves on the trail to get at the small pebbles exposed in the dirt by the stream of hikers. As I watched him, I pondered how turkeys are among the birds that must ingest small stones in order to digest their food. Possessing no teeth to crush the outer shell of the food they eat, their body chemistry depends upon the process whereby the ingested rocks grind up the food in order for it to nourish their bodies.

That's an appropriate metaphor for this process. We need to ingest the stones—the hard lessons—along with all the rest in order to be nourished and to continue growing. It's a natural part of the process. Think of any difficulties you encounter as you persevere to live these seven commonsense principles as the necessary stones to digest the learning and provide the nourishment you need to learn and grow.

In the Arabic culture they have this proverb. "All sunshine makes a desert." We can't always have sunshine. We need those storms to jar us, awaken our right brain, to challenge and shatter our old paradigms. The storms are a natural and necessary part of the journey. Sometimes we have to learn the hard way. Don't become frustrated and give up when you have struggles. The seven principles are your compass through the fog and the storms.

When I go hiking, there's one place I like best. It's not the mountaintop favored by most with its majestic views. Although I appreciate the beauty that can be enjoyed from that perspective, my favorite place on the hike is deep in the valley. As I wind down the trail deeper and deeper into the heart of the forest, I'm overcome by the calmness there. High above on the ridges and mountaintops the wind rages, whipping the trees into a frenzy. But in the valley where I am, it's calm and still. Against the backdrop of the blowing leaves and creaking branches and the trickling brook, I can almost hear the rhododendrons blooming and the fern fronds uncurling. This calm place in the forest is my favorite because it reminds me of that peaceful place deep inside me. Let the wind blow and the storms rage above me. I'm not deterred by any of it. I've made the journey and found that sweet spot of deep inner calm, peace, and joy. The seven commonsense principles can lead you to such a place of your own, if you're only willing to make the trip.

That's what I believe. That's the great gift freely given to me by all my wonderful teachers. That's the cure I would fight all obstacles to give to you. Be inspiring. Be a good coach and lifelong learner. Give unconditional love and acceptance. Be committed to a vision. Make a connection. Be structured and organized. Believe in others. Focus your life on this commonsense wisdom. Focus not on what you can get, but on what you can give to others through these seven principles, and you will miraculously find your own way.

For Further Information

Rhonda is dedicated to helping individuals and organizations create positive change, by applying her professional experience in strategic planning, culture-building, team-building, change management, instructional design & delivery, and facilitation. Her services can be engaged as a consultant, coach, teacher, and trainer. Standard programs are available, or Rhonda can tailor a custom program to your specific needs.

When to call for Rhonda's services:

Companies & Organizations
- When you want to learn how to use the seven principles to change the direction or culture of your organization.
- When your department or team needs to learn new skills together to improve communication, human interaction, and group dynamics.
- When you want your organization to work together at all levels to build better relationships and a more engaging workplace.
- When you want the author to speak at a meeting of your club or professional organization.

Teachers & Trainers
- When you want to learn how to apply the seven principles to be the most engaging and inspiring teacher or trainer you can be.
- When you want the seven principles presented in a guest lecture or as part of a curriculum.

Individuals
- When you want to clarify what's working well in your life & learn how to apply the seven principles to create more of what you want.

Rhonda Jones

Rhonda would like to hear how the seven principles enable your journey. By contacting her at the address below, please share the stories of how you experience *Teaching Common Sense* in your own life and the actions it prompts you to take.

You can also inquire about engaging Rhonda's services at this address. If you would like a written response, please send a stamped, self-addressed envelope.

Rhonda Jones
c/o Bright Hope Productions
Post Office Box 50730
Knoxville, Tennessee 37950

Check out Rhonda's online newsletter and calendar of events and learn more about the author on her website. Also preview Rhonda's forthcoming books in her *Common Sense Series*, addressing the topics of achieving balance in our approach to working and giving of our time, talents, and resources. A synopsis of *Working Common Sense* and *Giving Common Sense* can be found on the author's website, where you can also initiate electronic requests for services or further information: **www.rhondajones.us.**

CPSIA information can be obtained at www.ICGtesting.com
Printed in the USA
LVOW120931171111

255407LV00001B/269/A

9 780976 662402